Faith

God's Answer For Your Disappointments And Suffering

Daniel R. Jennings

SEAN
MULTIMEDIA

Faith: God's Answer For Your Disappointments And Suffering

Jennings, Daniel, R. 1977-
  Faith: God's Answer For Your Disappointments And Suffering.

ISBN-13: 978-1512335293
ISBN-10: 1512335290

Special thanks to those from the Covenant Marriage Standers Facebook group for their feedback.

www.seanmultimedia.com

οτι ουκ αδυνατησει παρα του θεου παν ρημα
Lucas I.XXXVII

Table Of Contents

Chapter 1:

Introduction

What do we do when life goes completely contrary to the way we feel it should? How do we handle life's disappointments, failures, bad news and let downs? In 2012 I became unemployed, lost my home and separated from my wife all within about a week's time. It was the culmination of a set of circumstances that had begun months (maybe years) earlier and, as bad as it seemed, was just the beginning of a much longer season of suffering in my life.

As I entered into the darkest period of my life (up until then) I was faced with many questions for which I had no answer: Where was God? Why had He abandoned me? What do I do? Who can help me?

All people suffer. But not all respond appropriately to their sufferings. For some, suffering turns to bitterness and unforgiveness towards God. For others it turns to despair and, sometimes, even suicide and we are led to ask the question how does one handle the big (and small) setbacks, hurts and disappointments that *we all* experience.

As I journeyed through the darkest night of my soul I discovered a way of looking at life that not only made sense of the suffering I was experiencing but helped me to see suffering in a way I had never seen it before as I looked at it through the lens of *faith*. And if you will allow me I would like to show you why no matter how hurtful your situation has been, there is good *behind* and *in* it and though you may have felt like God was nowhere to be found He was there with you all of the time.

Chapter 2:
What Is Faith?

Many books have been written on how to apply faith to suffering but most of these seem to miss the Bible's real message on faith. These books usually approach faith and suffering from the standpoint of "If you are suffering, then it is evidence that you do not have *enough* faith." While a lack of faith can certainly lead to more suffering, looking at faith only from that perspective misses out on a whole view of faith and life that God wants to impart to us.

Bible translators have chosen the English word *faith* to translate the Greek word *pistis*. The word *faith* in English carries with it the idea of "complete trust or confidence in someone or something", "firm belief in something", and "something that is believed especially with strong conviction". In essence, to have faith in something is to believe it to be true in one's heart, to have confidence that the thing in question is really real, and to be convinced that it is so.

The Bible defines faith as follows:

Now faith is the substance of things hoped for, the evidence of things not seen. Heb 11:1KJV

The Bible tells us that faith is the "substance" behind something we believe in, yet do not readily see. When we look at how other translations have translated this verse we see what faith is a little more clearly.

NIV: "...faith is confidence..."
ASV: "...faith is assurance..."
NET Bible: "...faith is being sure..."
Phillips: "...faith means putting our full confidence in..."

Faith is being sure of something and, as a result of that surety, putting our full confidence into it. But the question is, when we suffer *what* should we be placing our faith *in*? As I thought about this great mystery while trying to interpret my own grief and heartache I came to the conclusion that there were at least three things that we all need to place our faith in when we experience suffering: Faith that all experience suffering, faith that God is in control of our lives, and faith that God has good intentions for the suffering He has sent into our lives. These three areas of faith apply for every seemingly negative situation. From the indescribable grief of losing a child to the devastation of a cancer diagnosis, to the pain and heartache of divorce down to those minor frustrations such as being unhappy with your job or wondering why you don't have a date for Valentine's Day the message of faith in these three areas speaks to each of these situations. If you are tired of being frustrated and confused as to why everything that is happening to you is happening, I invite you to join me as we look for the answer to our sufferings in the message of faith.

Chapter 3:
Faith That All Suffer

All humans wonder why we suffer. While there are many differences between the men of the world (cultural, linguistic, physiological) the one thing that is universal is that life is going to have hurt, heartaches, setbacks and disappointments. However, not everyone realizes this to be the case. This is especially true when we are going through a difficult time ourselves. We look at our circumstances and we compare ourselves to people who are doing better than we and somehow reason that others don't really suffer. Deep down I think that we all know that no matter what we are going through, there is someone going through something worse but when we are focused on our own suffering we have a tendency to feel like we are worse off than others. The wife whose husband had left her looks at the couple across the street and says "Bob and Debbie never fight. Why is their life so free of suffering?" The man who has been diagnosed with cancer looks at his healthy coworker and says "Ron is a picture of health. Why has he been spared from trials?" The underemployed individual looks at his high paid boss and imagines that life would be so much better if he could get that kind of salary. And the list goes on and on. As humans, when we are going through a difficult time our eyes are naturally drawn to those who aren't and though we may deep down know differently doing this has the effect of making us feel like we are somehow outside of a special area of protection from all sufferings that exists for some people. But the truth is *all suffer* in some way or another.

All men born to women live only a few days and have lots of trouble. Job 14:1

Why Do We Suffer?
The Scriptures tell us that we all suffer as a consequence of Adam and Eve's disobedience in the garden. Most are familiar with how God placed the first man and woman into a perfect environment where they had the ability live forever in pleasure. The man and his wife, however, disobeyed God at the instigation of Satan and as a result God decreed that they and all of their

4

descendants would be forced to endure a life filled with hardship and suffering (Gen 3:1-24). God's curse on humanity resulted in the following universal proclamation by Him:

> To the woman He (God) said: "I will greatly multiply your sorrow and your conception; in pain you shall bring forth children; your desire shall be for your husband, and he shall rule over you." Then to Adam He said, "Because you have heeded the voice of your wife, and have eaten from the tree of which I commanded you, saying, 'You shall not eat of it': "Cursed is the ground for your sake; in toil you shall eat of it all the days of your life. Both thorns and thistles it shall bring forth for you, and you shall eat the herb of the field. In the sweat of your face you shall eat bread till you return to the ground, for out of it you were taken; for dust you are, and to dust you shall return." Gen 3:16-19

Adam and Eve went from a life of pleasureful and fulfilling industry to one of sorrow and hard labor. No longer would life be easy. No more would life be perfect. Life which was supposed to last forever (eternal life) now became temporary and the day Adam and Eve were expelled from the garden became the day that they began to age as they headed towards their deaths.

The Memory Serves As Hope

From the moment of their discipline the bliss of paradise became only a memory. For some the experience of losing something that can never be regained can become a *haunting memory*. We say "He was haunted by the loss of his wife" or "She was haunted by the loss of her career". Yet, for Adam and Eve (and all of their descendants) it is this very memory of paradise lost that actually serves to build our faith because somehow, deep inside of all of us, is this memory of the life that was lost in Eden and the hope that it can somehow be regained.

In the book of Romans Paul discusses the connection between the curse and suffering and how it pushes us to desire for what was lost in the Garden.

> For I consider that the sufferings of this present time are not worthy to be compared with the glory which shall be

5

revealed in us. For the earnest expectation of the creation eagerly waits for the revealing of the sons of God. For the creation was subjected to futility, not willingly, but because of Him who subjected it in hope; because the creation itself also will be delivered from the bondage of corruption into the glorious liberty of the children of God. For we know that the whole creation groans and labors with birth pangs together until now. Not only that, but we also who have the firstfruits of the Spirit, even we ourselves groan within ourselves, eagerly waiting for the adoption, the redemption of our body. For we were saved in this hope, but hope that is seen is not hope; for why does one still hope for what he sees? But if we hope for what we do not see, we eagerly wait for it with perseverance. Rom 8:18-25NKJV

A few points need to be emphasized from this passage.

For I consider that the sufferings of this present time are not worthy to be compared with the glory which shall be revealed in us. Rom 8:18NKJV

Paul begins this section by hinting to the fact that a time is coming in which suffering will come to an end and that this release from suffering is so wonderful that it will be incomparable to the sufferings that we have experienced in this life.

For the earnest expectation of the creation eagerly waits for the revealing of the sons of God...For we know that the whole creation groans and labors with birth pangs together until now. Not only that, but we also who have the firstfruits of the Spirit, even we ourselves groan within ourselves, eagerly waiting for the adoption, the redemption of our body. Rom 8:19, 22-23NKJV

Paul points out how that all of living creation secretly waits (hopes) for this time to come. No one enjoys suffering, not even animals and all of creation cries out and longs with earnestness for a release from our suffering. Deep down we all know that there is a release coming from this and all creation wants it.

6

For the creation was subjected to futility, not willingly, but because of Him who subjected it in hope; because the creation itself also will be delivered from the bondage of corruption into the glorious liberty of the children of God. Rom 8:20-21NKJV

Paul explained that creation was forced into weakness, not of its own will but by God who did it "in hope". What this means is that, even though God introduced suffering into the world, He only did so in such a way that mankind had a hope of one day escaping it. We see this hope expressed in God's declaration to the snake in the garden.

And the Lord God said unto the serpent, Because you have done this, you are cursed above all cattle, and above every beast of the field; upon your belly you shall go, and dust you shall eat all the days of your life: And I will put enmity between you and the woman, and between your seed and her seed; he shall bruise your head, and you shall bruise his heel. Gen 3:14-15

The snake was told that he would bruise the heel of the woman's descendant (a non-lethal wound) but the woman was told that her descendant would bruise the snake's head (a lethal wound). This statement carried with it more than just a reference to mankind's battle with snakes over the ages but pointed to how Eve's descendant Jesus, though wounded by Satan, would ultimately triumph over him in complete victory, undoing all that he had played a part in causing in the Garden (including the introduction of suffering into the world). So God, in His mercy, gave Adam and Eve a hope that what the snake had lured them into, one day He would undo. This is why Paul said in Romans above "For the creation was subjected to futility, not willingly, but because of Him who subjected it *in hope* ..."

Paul ends his passage by pointing out that salvation is based upon this hope being fulfilled.

For we were saved in this hope, but hope that is seen is not hope; for why does one still hope for what he sees? But if we hope for what we do not see, we eagerly wait for it with perseverance. Rom 8:24-25NKJV

So, if you are going through a period of suffering at this time in your life take hope—God has promised to bring an end to suffering for those who persevere in seeking Him.

Discipline vs. Revenge

There is a vast difference between discipline and revenge. Discipline is designed to make a person realize their bad choices and avoid repeating them. Revenge simply sets out to hurt or destroy the person with little to no concern for their personal well-being. God's decision to introduce suffering into the world was not revenge, but rather a *merciful discipline* whose end goal was to bring humanity back to Him.

This is really why there is suffering in the world. The suffering was not God's way of getting revenge for what Adam and Eve had done. Instead, it was His way of helping them to realize what disobeying Him results in and to serve as a means of drawing people back to Him. It is an observable fact that the more one suffers, the more likely they are to rely on God. Think about it, when are people more likely to pray—on a good day when everything is going right or on a bad day when everything is going wrong?

Even in the sending of death, we see the mercy of God. Think about this: God could have designed the dying process to work the opposite way than it does (i.e. we could struggle the most when we are young but then grow into vitality and youthful vigor). Instead He did just the opposite. The older we get (and naturally the closer we get to facing our judgment) the *weaker* we get. This was not a coincidence. God designed our sufferings that result from the aging-dying process so that the closer we get to the time of our death the more *we have to* rely on Him to handle life. When we are young we go where we want to go, do what we want to do and generally do not have to think about God for help doing things physically. But the older we get the harder it is to go where we want to go and do the things that we want to do. Aging brings with it all kinds of challenges—*trouble getting up, trouble walking, trouble remembering, trouble taking care of ourselves*. The aging-dying process literally forces us into a position to where our

8

natural inclination will be to cry out to God for help. This is a clear example of the mercy of God who sends suffering to draw us to Him, not to get revenge.

The Purpose Of Suffering

The purpose of suffering, then, is seen to be to help us realize our need for God in our lives. We were created to walk in relationship and fellowship with God but our natural tendency is to try and live on our own without God. However, when we are faced with weaknesses these teach us to depend on God because we cry out to Him for help and we see Him help us in our time of need. These experiences are all orchestrated by God, who sends them to help us learn who He is. This, then, is the purpose of suffering in the world—*to lead us back to God*—and is the reason that you and I have all of the sufferings that we ever have or ever will experience. The purpose of suffering is to help us find God.

Chapter 4:

Faith That God Is In Control Of All Suffering

Once we realize that suffering is a normal part of life we must have faith that God, the Creator of the Universe, is *in control* of all suffering. For many people this is a difficult belief to accept because we have trouble thinking of God as being responsible for negative things. We think of Him only as a God who blesses, not one who brings disaster. But, according to the Bible, both blessing and curse actually come from God. Our triumphs are just as much from Him as are our tragedies. The best way to prove this is to simply show that the Bible says that God not only controls *all suffering* but He controls *all other things*.

The Sovereignty Of God

When we talk about the "sovereignty" of God we mean that He is in complete control *over* and *of* every situation that occurs. For many this is a difficult concept to grasp because we have adopted the clockmaker view of God. In this view God is seen as a clock-maker who builds a clock (the universe) but then sets back and lets it run itself. Once the clock is built and running it may encounter problems (broken springs, damage from natural elements, etc.) that affect its performance. In this scenario the clock is built by God but other external forces have a negative effect on it. Nothing could be further from the truth! Not only did God build the universe but He also controls and guides every detail of it, including all of the external forces that have a negative effect on you and me.

The simplest way to express this is to just say that God controls *everything* that happens—everything!!! And we can easily demonstrate this by looking at a few verses which say this.

According to the Bible, we make plans for our life but the Lord directs the way our life will go:

A man's heart devises his way: but the Lord directs his steps. Pro 16:9

There are many devices in a man's heart; nevertheless the counsel of the Lord, that is what will stand. Pro 19:21

We come up with all kinds of plans for our lives. We say I am going to have a successful career by 25, a spouse and kids by 30, my house paid off by 50, etc., etc. but it often doesn't work out that way. We can make plans all day long and into the night but it's ultimately God who decides what direction our lives will go in.

No matter what you and I try to do, it will never override what God decides to do:

The Lord of hosts hath sworn, saying, Surely **as I have thought**, so shall it come to pass; and **as I have purposed**, so shall it stand. Isa 14:24KJV

It's not according to what we purpose or think that determines what happens in our lives. It is totally based upon *what God thinks and purposes to happen*. I can think and purpose all day long that when I wake up tomorrow I am going to be a millionaire but unless God decides for it to happen, my thinking and purposing is not going to accomplish anything.

According to the Scriptures today, like every other day, was made by God:

This is the day which the Lord has made; we will rejoice and be glad in it. Psa 118:24

The Psalmist here is referring to the coming of Jesus into the world (vs.22) but this verse is really applicable to every day because no day would occur unless God Himself made it. Just as you and I knit together a sweater, so God knitted together the events that took place in the world today. The Lord literally "made" this day what it was. This includes everything from the big things such as deciding what natural disasters would occur all the way down to the seemingly little and insignificant things, such as which of the billions of birds around the world are going to breathe their last breath.

Are not two sparrows sold for a copper coin? And not one of them falls to the ground apart from your Father's will. Mat 10:29NKJV

According to Jesus, not even a seemingly unimportant bird dies unless God decides that He wants that bird to die. Scientists estimate that there are as many as 400 billion birds in the world and God is so focused on *each of them* that not a single one of them will ever die without His approval first. That is incredible! What that shows us is that God is far more involved in the affairs of the world than most realize. And if God is so involved with the affairs of birds, *how could He not be involved in the much more important affairs that affect your life every day?*

What most do not realize is that before you and I were even born God had already made a plan for our lives.

You saw me before I was born. Every day of my life was recorded in your book. Every moment was laid out before a single day had passed. Psa 139:16NLT

This is why God told some people that the things they ended up doing for Him were already decided before they had even been born:

Before I formed you in the belly I knew you; and before you came forth out of the womb I sanctified you, and I ordained you a prophet unto the nations. Jer 1:5

But when it pleased God, who separated me from my mother's womb, and called me by his grace, to reveal his Son in me, that I might preach him among the heathen; I did not immediately confer with flesh and blood: Gal 1:15-16

The Lord has called me from the womb; from the bowels of my mother he has made mention of my name. Isa 49:1b

Before you were even born God was already guiding the affairs of your life, deciding who you would be born to, knitting

12

your little body together and deciding what environment you would be born into and raised in.

The understanding that God guides the lives of *every person* can be seen by looking at how Paul introduced the Gospel to the citizens of Athens. Paul was faced with a unique challenge. In Athens he found men and women who had never heard of the true God and he wanted to best present who the Creator and Sustainer of the universe was to them. He wanted the people to understand that the real God (unlike the Greco-Roman false gods) desired an intimate and personal relationship with every human being. So how did he do this? He did it by introducing Him as a Being who had always been involved in their lives, guiding and directing their daily affairs with the intent that the circumstances He sent into their lives would encourage them to seek out and find Him:

> God that made the world and all things therein, seeing that he is Lord of heaven and earth, does not dwell in temples made with hands; neither is he worshipped with men's hands, as though he needed anything, seeing he gives to all life, and breath, and all things. And has made of one blood every nation of men to dwell on all the face of the earth, having determined allotted periods and the boundaries of their habitation; so that they should seek the Lord, in the hope that they might feel after him, and find him, though he is not far from every one of us: Act 17:24-27

There are two important parts to Paul's theology of the Sovereignty of God here. First, according to Paul when God created the world He "determined allotted periods" for the nations of men including the "boundaries of their habitation". This means that when God wanted the Babylonian Empire to flourish, it flourished. Then, when He was ready for it to be replaced by the Persian Empire, Cyrus the Great was allowed to conquer Babylon. Then when He was ready for the Persians to collapse, He raised up Alexander the Great to establish the Greek Empire and so on and so forth until we come to our own times. The same has been true for all nations of all times. They only existed and they only encompassed the geographical land mass that they conquered because God decided that they would do that. Every country that exists does so because God wants it to.

Secondly, and here is the most important part, God did all of this so "that they should seek the Lord, in the hope that they might feel after him, and find him". And this is very important in helping us to realize the message of faith. What this is saying is that every nation which exists was created by God for the specific purpose of helping people to find Him. This means that whatever country a person was born in, they were put there by God for the explicit purpose that he or she would find God by their experience of living in that country. This means that *you* were born in the country you were born in because God decided that this would be the best place for you to find Him. For some people, He deems that it would be best for them to find Him while growing up in China. For others, England works best. For some, the U.S. and so forth. What this means is that while you could have been born in any of the world's nearly 200 countries, God decided that you could find Him best right where you were born. And this brings us back to the point we were making in chapter three about how when God expelled Adam and Eve out of the Garden and introduced suffering His intent from the beginning was to draw people back to Him. The plain and simple truth is that you and I are where we are because God put us there. (And this includes any negative circumstances or consequences that you find yourself in).

This is why the Bible says that God is working out *everything that happens* in the world for His purposes. It's because He is controlling everything (the big and the small), guiding it to the fulfilment of His perfect plan for it.

In whom also we have obtained an inheritance, being predestinated according to the purpose of him who *works all things* after the counsel of his own will: Eph 1:11

God works "all things" in your and my life in accordance with His own plans and purposes. Everything that happens to you and I is a part of His will for us, to help bring about the end result that He desires.

A lot of people will object to saying that God controls everything because they cannot believe that God would ever cause anything *bad* to happen. While people who feel this way can be

14

good intentioned, to see God as only responsible for the good is to misrepresent how He is presented in the Scriptures.

> Consider the work of God: who can make straight what he has made crooked? In the day of prosperity be joyful, and in the day of adversity consider: **God has made the one as well as the other**, so that man may not find out anything that will be after him. Ecc 7:13-14ESV

If you are having a good and prosperous day, God made it for you! We don't normally have a problem accepting that. However, notice what else Solomon says:

> In the day of prosperity be joyful, and **in the day of adversity consider: God has made the one as well as the other**…

Solomon says that God also *makes* the day of adversity. What this means is that our *bad days* come from God also. That's a real revelation for a lot of people but it goes in tandem with what we have been saying. Namely, that God sends us suffering to help us realize our need for Him. Solomon points out that on good days we can be joyful but notice also how he says that in the day of adversity we should *consider* how that God also sends those days.

One reason we should *consider* the bad days is because God always orchestrates our trials with a purpose in mind. All people have a certain amount of closeness or knowledge of God. This does not mean that all are saved or in fellowship with Him but it does mean that everyone knows in their heart that God exists and some live more close to Him in thought and action than others. When we go through bad times, these experiences help us to realize the ways that we are not close enough to God and the areas that we lack knowledge of Him in. It is through our bad times that God helps us to realize, overcome and grow in those areas that He wants us to change in:

> Not only that, but we rejoice in our sufferings, knowing that suffering produces endurance, and endurance produces character, and character produces hope, and hope does not put us to shame, because God's love has been poured into

our hearts through the Holy Spirit who has been given to us. Rom 5:3-5ESV

My brethren, count it all joy when you fall into various trials, knowing that the testing of your faith produces patience. Jam 1:2-3NKJV

When we go through bad days those days are actually *designed* and *orchestrated* by God to help us become better people. God has made the nature of suffering such that it operates in such a way as to help us become stronger and improved people. This is why we should question why we are having a bad day when one occurs. That is, we should ask what lesson is God trying to teach us about and what area does He want to change in us through what we are going through.

I feel like some people are going to resist the idea that God actually gives us our bad days so I want to share a few other Scriptures that essentially say the same thing.

According to the Bible all that God has to do is speak for something to happen. (Well, He can probably just think and make it happen, but the point is that unlike you and me whatever He says *will* happen). This is why Paul says that God "calls into existence the things that do not exist (Rom 4:17ESV)". He simply speaks it forth and it comes to pass. This is demonstrated clearly in the book of Genesis where it says over and over again that all God did was speak and things came into being:

And God **_said_**, Let there be light: and there was light…And God **_said_**, Let the waters under the heaven be gathered together unto one place, and let the dry land appear: and it was so…And God **_said_**, Let the earth bring forth grass…And the earth brought forth grass… (Gen 1:3,9,11-12)

That being demonstrated, we can now understand what God says in the book of Lamentations:

Who has spoken and it came to pass, unless the Lord has commanded it? Is it not from the mouth of the Most High that good and bad come? Lam 3:37-38ESV

16

Good and bad (all good and bad) that comes into our lives does so because God decrees that it should be. Jeremiah directly tells us above that when good and bad come they *both* originate from the spoken decree of God who alone decides what will and will not happen—whether our day will be good or our day will be bad.

But to make it even clearer we just need to look at Isaiah where God says through the prophet that:

I create the light and make the darkness. **I send good times and bad times. I, the LORD, am the one who does these things**. Isa 45:7NLT

Although we might struggle with it, God Himself has declared that *He is the one* who sends both the good and the bad times that we experience. They both come from God.

Some will look at things like Pearl Harbor or September 11th and say did God really do that? Is He really the cause of disasters like that? If we believe the Bible, then we have to say "Yes, God caused even that." To confirm this we see that as God was speaking through the prophet Amos He rhetorically asked the people:

Is a trumpet blown in a city, and the people are not afraid?
Does disaster come to a city, unless the Lord has done it?
Amo 3:6ESV

The answer was obvious. Since God controlled everything, and disaster could only come because He spoke it into existence, then disaster would *never* come to a city unless the Lord had caused it. The plain and simple truth is that God controls all of the things that happen to you and I and *nothing* happens to you or I unless God *wants* it to happen to us.

What About The Devil?

People who have never been taught about the sovereignty of God will naturally ask "What about Satan?" Well, he certainly exists and he certainly plays a part in much of the evil that occurs in the world but even he is *completely under the control* of God.

He is never allowed to do anything that God does not want him to do and, like all others, Satan's actions are used by God to achieve His purposes on the earth. To prove this we will look at a few examples from the Bible.

First, when Job was afflicted by Satan we see that Satan first *had to get God's permission* to do what he did to him.

Now there was a day when the sons of God came to present themselves before the Lord, and Satan also came among them. And the Lord said to Satan, "From where do you come?" So Satan answered the Lord and said, "From going to and fro on the earth, and from walking back and forth on it." Then the Lord said to Satan, "Have you considered My servant Job, that there is none like him on the earth, a blameless and upright man, one who fears God and shuns evil?" So Satan answered the Lord and said, "Does Job fear God for nothing? **Have You not made a hedge around him, around his household, and around all that he has on every side?** You have blessed the work of his hands, and his possessions have increased in the land. But now, stretch out Your hand and touch all that he has, and he will surely curse You to Your face!" And the Lord said to Satan, "Behold, **all that he has is in your power**; only do not lay a hand on his person." So Satan went out from the presence of the Lord. Job 1:6-12NKJV

When we look at the conversation between Satan and God it is easy to see that *God controls all that Satan does*. When Satan accused Job before God he pointed out that God had put a "*hedge around him, around his household, and around all that he has on every side*" indicating that there was nothing that he (Satan) could do to him. Satan's power was restrained by God and he could do nothing to Job (or anyone else) without God allowing him to do it. Before Satan could do anything to Job God had to first explicitly tell him that "*all that he has is in your power*". And it was only *after* God did this that Satan was able to cause problems in Job's life (not before). And the same is true for every other person who has ever lived when it comes to Satan. Satan is never able to do anything to you or me unless God first approves it.

18

The idea that God is responsible for everything, even what the Devil does, is demonstrated even clearer in Job's discussion of his trials with his wife:

His wife said to him, "You are still as faithful as ever, aren't you? Why don't you curse God and die?" Job answered, "You are talking nonsense! When God sends us something good, we welcome it. How can we complain when **he** sends us trouble?" Job 2:9-10bGNT

Even though the text clearly says that Satan is the one who brought Job his troubles, he understood that all things ultimately originate from and are under the control of God. So, Job didn't give the power to Satan but he rightly ascribed it to God, who controls all things. Therefore, even when Satan brings trouble, it is Biblical to say that God is the one who sent it.

Secondly, we see that God even uses Satan to accomplish His purposes in the earth. The Scriptures clearly say that it was God's will and God's plan for Jesus to die for the sins of humanity so that He might become the atoning sacrifice for the sins of the world (Act 2:22-23, Luk 22:41-43, 1Jn 2:2). And when we look at Satan's role in the circumstances that led up to Jesus' death what do we see?

Now before the Feast of the Passover, when Jesus knew that His hour had come that He should depart from this world to the Father, having loved His own who were in the world, He loved them to the end. And supper being ended, **the devil having already put it into the heart of Judas Iscariot**, Simon's son, to betray Him, Jesus…was troubled in spirit, and testified and said, "Most assuredly, I say to you, one of you will betray Me…It is he to whom I shall give a piece of bread when I have dipped it." And having dipped the bread, He gave it to Judas Iscariot, the son of Simon. Now after the piece of bread, **Satan entered him**. Then Jesus said to him, "What you do, do quickly." Jhn 13:1-3, 21, 26-27NKJV

Pay close attention to what is happening here. God wanted Jesus to die and *He used Satan* to accomplish what He wanted.

Remember that the Bible teaches that God "works all things after the counsel of his own will (Eph 1:11)", even the activities of Satan. Satan never does anything that God does not ultimately want him to do. He cannot do anything to you or I without it being the express will of God that he do so. Now, one might ask, does Satan realize that he is ultimately working to fulfill God's will? He probably doesn't. Just like the majority of humans who have no idea that they are being used by God to fulfill His plan, the Devil probably doesn't either—yet like everyone else he is used by God to bring about the things in this earth that He wants to happen (as is clearly demonstrated in the death of Jesus).

Finally, let's talk a little about demons (evil spirits). If we will look closely at the Scriptures, we will see that even these beings (the spirits of fallen angels) are used by God. While many people have been taught to think of evil spirits as out of the control of God, they actually work for Him.

Now Abimelech ruled over Israel three years. **Then God sent an evil spirit between Abimelech and the men of Shechem**; and the men of Shechem dealt treacherously with Abimelech, so that the violence done to the seventy sons of Jerubbaal might come, and their blood might be laid on Abimelech their brother, who killed them, and on the men of Shechem, who strengthened his hands to kill his brothers. Jdg 9:22-24NASB

In the above situation, God was angry because Abimelech had murdered his seventy brothers with the support of the Shechemites and in order to punish them both, the Bible says that the Lord sent an evil spirit to incite the Shechemites into war against him. It clearly says that "_God_ sent an evil spirit". It wasn't the Devil who sent him. It wasn't the spirit just going around looking for ways to cause trouble. No, it was God who sent the evil spirit that started the war and it was all so that it might bring about His purpose of punishing Abimelech and the Shechemites for their wickedness. Other examples will help to demonstrate this.

Now the Lord's Spirit departed from Saul, and an evil spirit from the Lord troubled him. 1Sa 16:14

20

In the above example, King Saul had backslidden from the Lord and as a result an evil spirit troubled him. Who does the Bible say sent the evil spirit to Saul? It clearly says that "an evil spirit *from the Lord*" came to him. It wasn't from Satan. It wasn't the evil spirit's own decision. It was God who sent the evil spirit.

In our final example we look at the story of King Ahab. Ahab was a wicked king and God decided that He would punish Ahab for his wickedness by allowing him to be defeated and die in battle. God gave His servant Micaiah a vision of how He was going to punish Ahab for his wickedness and in the vision Micaiah was allowed to see how God sovereignly controls all things, in part by using evil spirits to accomplish His will in the earth. What follows is Micaiah's description of his vision demonstrating this:

> I saw the LORD sitting on his throne, and all the army of heaven standing by him on his right hand and on his left. The LORD said, 'Who will entice Ahab, that he may go up and fall at Ramoth Gilead?' One said one thing; and another said another. **A spirit came out and stood before the LORD, and said, 'I will entice him.'** The LORD said to him, 'How?' He said, 'I will go out and will be **a lying spirit in the mouth of all his prophets**.' He said, 'You will entice him, and will also prevail. Go out and do so.' 1Ki 22:19-22

In the above vision God asks His heavenly court who will play a part in bringing about Ahab's downfall. Different suggestions are made until finally a spirit suggests that he be allowed to go down to the earth and inspire the false prophets that Ahab trusts in to prophesy that he will be victorious in battle. This will give him confidence to go up and fight. God gives the spirit permission to go and sends him to do this. If you read the whole story you will see that the spirit inspires the false prophets to give Ahab a false confidence and he goes up to battle where he dies as a punishment for his sins. The passage above clearly shows that it is God who sent the spirit to accomplish this. It wasn't Satan who sent the evil spirit to inspire the false prophets. It was God who sent him in order to bring about His plan, purpose and will for the situation.

21

Even in the stories of demoniacs in the New Testament what do we see? We see that every demon obeyed whatever Jesus told them to do and their having been allowed to possess the people that they did served to encourage the eyewitnesses to trust in Jesus. God clearly used the demons in the ministry of Jesus to encourage people to believe in Him as the Son of God.

The bottom line of the story is that God controls everyone and everything and no one operates outside of His plan and purpose for the earth. No matter how wicked or rebellious a person (or angelic being) may be, they will only fulfill God's plan and purpose in this universe. It has always been that way and it always will be.

This also means that we do not have to be afraid of the Devil or demons. They cannot do anything to us that God does not allow them to do. We need only fear God (Mat 10:28) as He may use them to discipline or punish us but there is nothing in and of the demons themselves that we have to be afraid of for they can do nothing to us outside of God's will.

Does Mankind Have Freewill?

The belief that God controls all things does not negate the idea of freewill. Mankind obviously has some level of free will or else there would be no purpose or logic behind God's method of rewards and punishments for the life we live (Rom 2:1-11). But the fact that you and I do have some level of freewill does not mean that God cannot control everything that happens. In actuality, God is so big and so powerful that not only can He give you and I freewill but He can also control everything that happens at the same time. And that just makes God even bigger than many of us had previously realized. You can rest assured that while you and I do have a limited ability to choose the wrong thing, those choices on our part will never be allowed to bring hurt or suffering to someone else without it being part of God's plan for that person's life.

Chapter 5:
Faith In The Goodness Of God

By this point you have probably grown (at least somewhat) in your faith to believe that God controls everything but you may be struggling in another faith area now. At this point many will ask, *"If God controls everything, then how could He really be good, seeing as He is the one who is responsible for every hurt and heartache that I have ever suffered?"*

We already demonstrated that God created suffering to help us (who are all guilty of rebellion against Him) to stop rebelling and learn to trust in and rely on Him. This is certainly evidence of the loving nature of our Creator because we can see that He has taken steps to prod us in the right direction when a God who didn't care would not spend time doing that. But I would like to press this point on just a little further. Many people (myself included) know what it is like to doubt (lose faith) in the goodness of God during our times of suffering. When life is going great it's easy to believe and proclaim that God is good. We often hear people say "God is good!" when they get good news and they say this with complete faith. But what about when we get bad news? In my observation, people are not as likely to say that same thing.

But even when we get bad news, God is still *just as good* as when we got the good news. And to help build your faith up in this I want to show you how the Bible describes God.

The Bible clearly describes God as being a *good* Being.

Give thanks to the LORD, for **He is good**; His faithful love endures forever. Psa 107:1HCSB

The Psalmist clearly portrays God as a good God who does good to others.

You are good and do good; teach me your statutes. Psa 119:68

And this goodness of the Lord extends to all people.

The LORD is good to **all**, and his mercy is over all that he has made. Psa 145:9ESV

And here is the key, *because He is good*, He instructs us in the way that we should live:

Good and upright is the Lord; Therefore He instructs sinners in the way. Psa 25:8NASB

Notice what the Psalmist says. He first says that God is "Good and upright" and *because of this* "He instructs sinners in the way" that they should live. Take notice of this. This verse clearly says that it is *because* God is good that He teaches us how to live. And how does He do this? We answered it earlier. He instructs us by sending suffering into our lives! These sufferings in turn push us towards Him, drawing us into a closer fellowship and relationship with Him until we finally become the people that He wants us to be. So, what we see is that the very reason that many people accuse God of *not* being good (i.e. suffering in their lives) is actually a manifestation of His goodness.

God cares about the world and only wants the best for it. He gets no pleasure from sending death and suffering into your or my life.

"For I have no pleasure in the death of anyone who dies," declares the Lord GOD. "Therefore, repent and live." Ezk 18:32NASB

God is not some kind of sadistic monster god who sits in the Heavens and dreams up ways to torture His creation. That is just a total misrepresentation of God but how many of us (myself included) have sat back and accused God of getting some kind of satisfaction or enjoyment out of making us suffer? I know what it is like to be in prayer and to tell God that I think He is enjoying what I am going through. That somehow He is just having fun with all that He is putting me through. This, of course, was totally wrong (wrong of me to do and a wrong assumption on my part) but I feel like this is a common feeling that many people have. But if we do believe this way then how are we going to reconcile this not only with how the Bible describes God as a God of love but also with His demonstration of that love in sending Jesus?

He that does not love does not know God; for God is love. 1Jn 4:8

For God so loved the world, that he gave his only begotten Son, that whosoever believeth in him should not perish, but have everlasting life. Jhn 3:16KJV

But God commends his love toward us, in that, while we were still sinners, Christ died for us. Rom 5:8

As we noted earlier, it is the love of God towards humanity that actually pushes us into sufferings to help us realize the wrong choices that we have made:

The LORD is good and upright; *therefore* He shows sinners the way. Psa 25:8HCSB

Our sufferings are only designed and sent to help us become the people that God wants us to be and, therefore, to ultimately produce good in our lives. This is specifically stated to be so for the believer:

And we know that all things work together for good to them that love God, to them who are the called according to his purpose. Rom 8:28KJV

If you think about it, it has to work this way. How could God be good, yet do something (anything) bad? It's impossible. Logic and common sense compel us to accept this. Either God is *entirely* good or else He is *not* good because one cannot be good and bad at the same time.

Rest assured my friend that if you are going through sufferings that your sufferings are totally under the control of God and *only* sent for your good!

Realizing that all suffering is sent to help us become better people should encourage us to seek God in a special way during our trials. When we go through suffering and bad days we should pray and ask God to reveal to us why He sent the suffering. There could be a variety of reasons for the suffering. Sometimes, only God knows but if we sincerely ask Him for wisdom about our trials He promises to give it to us:

> If any of you lacks wisdom, let him ask God, who gives generously to all without reproach, and it will be given him. Jam 1:5ESV

So, if you are going through difficult times, don't be afraid to ask God to show you why you are experiencing it and then respond appropriately to what He shows you.

Chapter 6:
Review And Practical Applications

Now that we have looked at the three areas of faith let's do a brief review before proceeding onto some practical applications of the message of faith.

- First, we must have faith that everybody suffers and that suffering is just a normal part of life because of Adam and Eve's sin.
- Secondly, we must have faith that God controls all things and that *nothing* happens to you or I unless God decides that it should happen.
- Finally, we must have faith that God is a *good* God and, therefore, since He controls all suffering will only allow it to occur in our lives for a *good* purpose.

Having faith as it is defined above will cause some major changes in our way of thinking, change how we view certain verses in the Bible and help us to better understand some of the more seemingly "impossible" commandments in the Scriptures. Let's now look at the practical applications of living life with this kind of faith.

You Do Not Want A Perfect Life

Everybody wants a perfect life and we have a tendency to covet the lives and lifestyles of those whom we see with an easy life. But after realizing that God uses suffering to draw us to Him we realize that we shouldn't envy those who have such a life because the absence of suffering is an indication that God has given up on trying to draw that person to Him. In other words, since God universally uses suffering to draw people to Him, if a person never suffers it is evidence that God has stopped trying to draw that person to Him. *And you don't want to be that person!*

God universally sends circumstances to draw all men to Him but, sadly, not all men respond to these circumstances. The Scriptures indicate that there can come a point to where a person, after resisting God's drawing, will be given over to a deluded mind that thinks they are okay with God when in reality they are not. This is what Paul was talking about when He described how people in the last days would be given over to a "delusion" to worship the Antichrist and he explained that God did this to them *because* they refused to love righteousness:

> And then the lawless one (i.e. the Antichrist) will be revealed, whom the Lord will consume with the breath of His mouth and destroy with the brightness of His coming. The coming of the lawless one is according to the working of Satan, with all power, signs, and lying wonders, and with all unrighteous deception among those who perish, because they did not receive the love of the truth, that they might be saved. And for this reason God will send them strong delusion, that they should believe the lie, that they all may be condemned who did not believe the truth but had pleasure in unrighteousness. 2Th 2:8-12NKJV, parentheses added

Paul says that in the last days the Antichrist will be revealed and be allowed to come onto the scene "with all power, signs and lying wonders". Miracles are very persuasive at convincing people to believe something and the Bible indicates that people will see these supposed "miracles" and worship the Antichrist (Rev 13:1-14). But Paul explains that God only allows this to happen because these people had already refused to believe the truth and instead had pleasure in unrighteousness:

> And for this reason **God will send them strong delusion**, that they should believe the lie, that they all may be condemned who did not believe the truth but had pleasure in unrighteousness. 2Th 2:11-12NKJV

Notice that it is God who sends the delusion of the Antichrist as a man who seemingly has god-like powers. God does not send the Antichrist with supposed miracle working power because He wants to lead astray people who are well intentioned. No, He sends him as a judgment against people who have *already* rejected Him in their lives. And the same has been true all

28

throughout history. When men and women reject God from their lives, as a judgment He will allow them to come under a delusion—*a blindness*—that makes them think that they are okay with Him when in reality they are lost. Paul further elaborated on this in the book of Romans.

He begins by saying that it angers God that people reject the truth because He has made the difference between right and wrong initially obvious to everyone:

> For the wrath of God is revealed from heaven against all ungodliness and unrighteousness of men, who suppress the truth in unrighteousness, because what may be known of God is manifest in them, for God has shown it to them. For since the creation of the world His invisible attributes are clearly seen, being understood by the things that are made, even His eternal power and Godhead, so that they are without excuse... Rom 1:18-20NKJV

Even though they know the truth, mankind often rejects it and *as a result* their thinking becomes useless and their hearts darkened:

> ...because, although they knew God, they did not glorify Him as God, nor were thankful, but became futile in their thoughts, and their foolish hearts were darkened. Rom 1:21NKJV

In his explanation, Paul goes on to give the example of how people replace God with idols but, really, any rejection of God's truth in favor of a lie is no different and the result of persisting in this behavior will always ultimately be the same—*The experience of God giving us up to do what we want to do and the accompanying darkened and deceived mind that begins to tell us that what we are doing is okay*:

> Professing to be wise, they became fools, and changed the glory of the incorruptible God into an image made like corruptible man—and birds and four-footed animals and creeping things. Therefore **God also gave them up** to uncleanness, in the lusts of their hearts, to dishonor their

bodies among themselves, who exchanged the truth of God for the lie, and worshiped and served the creature rather than the Creator, who is blessed forever. Amen. For this reason **God gave them up to vile passions**. For even their women exchanged the natural use for what is against nature. Likewise also the men, leaving the natural use of the woman, burned in their lust for one another, men with men committing what is shameful, and receiving in themselves the penalty of their error which was due. And even as they did not like to retain God in their knowledge, **God gave them over to a debased mind**, to do those things which are not fitting; being filled with all unrighteousness, sexual immorality, wickedness, covetousness, maliciousness; full of envy, murder, strife, deceit, evil-mindedness; they are whisperers, backbiters, haters of God, violent, proud, boasters, inventors of evil things, disobedient to parents, undiscerning, untrustworthy, unloving, unforgiving, unmerciful; who, knowing the righteous judgment of God, that those who practice such things are deserving of death, not only do the same but also approve of those who practice them. Rom 1:22-32NKJV

In the above passage Paul is describing the process by which a person is given over to this kind of delusional thinking as a judgment. Notice that he clearly says that God is the one giving them over to their confused and deluded way of thinking. It has to be God who does this because, as we noted before, God controls everything. And once a person is given over to this darkened way of thinking, they are sometimes used by God to do even more wicked things to help bring about His ultimate plans for the world. We can see this clearly in the case of Pharaoh in the book of Exodus. Pharaoh was a man who had rejected God's will for his life because he abused other people, in his case the Hebrews by forcing them to become his slaves. He was obviously a wicked man because only an evil man would treat other people that way. And, just as Paul described in Romans, look at what God did to him:

So the Lord said to Moses: "See, I have made you as God to Pharaoh, and Aaron your brother shall be your prophet.

You shall speak all that I command you. And Aaron your brother shall tell Pharaoh to send the children of Israel out of his land. **And I will harden Pharaoh's heart**, and multiply My signs and My wonders in the land of Egypt. But Pharaoh will not heed you, so that I may lay My hand on Egypt and bring My armies and My people, the children of Israel, out of the land of Egypt by great judgments. Exd 7:1-4NKJV

God doesn't just take people and force them into sin. That would be completely contrary to the nature of God. But when a person has already turned their heart against God, he or she can become a tool in His hand to be used for His ultimate plan for the world. Such is the case of Pharaoh who was *already* a wicked person and, because of that, God hardened his heart so that he would further fight against God and ultimately end up being used to show the world how great and powerful God really was (Rom 9:17). In the end God's Name was magnified because it was shown that He was more powerful than all of Egypt's gods and this all happened in connection with the way Pharaoh was made to behave. The more Moses asked Pharaoh to free the Hebrew slaves, the more resistant Pharaoh was made to become. The more he resisted, the greater miracle God used to show how powerful He was. In the end God won, the Hebrews were freed, Egypt was left in ruins and Pharaoh went down in history as just one of many examples of men who rejected God and were given over to a depraved mind as a result.

The book of Revelation talks about a similar case where ten wicked kings, symbolically represented by horns, form an alliance with the Antichrist (symbolically described as a beast) and experience their own hearts being hardened by God.

"The ten horns which you saw are ten kings who have received no kingdom as yet, but they receive authority for one hour as kings with the beast (i.e. the Antichrist). These are of one mind, and they will give their power and authority to the beast. These will make war with the Lamb, and the Lamb will overcome them, for He is Lord of lords and King of kings; and those who are with Him are called, chosen, and faithful." Then he said to me, "The waters

31

which you saw, where the harlot sits, are peoples, multitudes, nations, and tongues. And the ten horns which you saw on the beast, these will hate the harlot, make her desolate and naked, eat her flesh and burn her with fire. **For God has put it into their hearts to fulfill His purpose, to be of one mind, and to give their kingdom to the beast**, until the words of God are fulfilled." Rev 17:12-17NKJV, parentheses added

The above last days' kings are clearly antichristian (the text says that they will actually fight against the spotless Lamb of God, Jesus Christ, and attempt to make war with Him). But look at what the last verse says about Who it is that makes them support the Antichrist:

For **God has put it into their hearts to fulfill His purpose, to be of one mind, and to give their kingdom to the beast**, until the words of God are fulfilled. Rev 17:17NKJV

It is God who put it in their hearts to fulfill His will and to agree with and place themselves under the authority of the Antichrist. It's not their own will (they lost that long before when they rejected God's will for their lives and came under the delusion).

One of the ways that God sends delusion on people is to give them an easy, perfect life. We have a tendency (a very mistaken tendency) to assume that if God is blessing us, that that means that we are right with Him. This was the mistaken thinking of Job's friends who all seemed intent on persuading him that his problems were the result of his sins because God didn't send bad things to good people and, likewise, God only sent good things to good people. But this way of thinking ignores what Jesus clearly taught. Jesus clearly said that God blesses *both* the wicked and the righteous:

But I say to you, Love your enemies and pray for those who persecute you, so that you may be sons of your Father who is in heaven. For he makes his sun rise on the evil and

on the good, and sends rain on the just and on the unjust.
Mat 5:44-45ESV

Jesus lived in a mostly agricultural society and it was of the utmost importance that people who live this way have both sun and rain, otherwise their crops won't grow and they will starve to death. Jesus was teaching us that we should be a blessing to those who hurt us and He did so by pointing out how that God did the same thing. God sends the blessing of sun and rain to both saints and sinners alike, blessing them so that they can live. What this means is that just because a person is blessed by God that does not mean that they are right with God. Even wicked people experience the regular blessing of God in their lives. But we have a tendency to think differently. When things are going great, we feel like we are right with God because we reason "Why would God bless me so much if He wasn't happy with me?" In some cases, God is blessing people as part of the delusion that He has sent them as a judgment. God knows how people think. He knows that if people have an easy, care-free life that they will think that He is pleased with Him and not take their salvation too seriously. This appears to be the judgment of untold millions of people in the world (especially in America where people think that because they live in the most blessed nation in the world that God is pleased with how they are living).

To demonstrate how a perfect life does not lead people to God we need only look at the religious beliefs of some of the world's richest men. There is no denying that the more money one has, the easier life will generally be. This is not always the case, but in general, wealth keeps people from experiencing many of the problems that plague less fortunate men (and the fewer problems one has the less they will be reminded of their need for God). When we look at the religious beliefs of some of the world's richest men do we see men who are wholeheartedly seeking the will of God in their lives? Bill Gates is the world richest man. Once, when asked about religion he replied, "There's a lot more I could be doing on a Sunday morning."[1] George Soros is worth an

---

[1] Walter Isaacson. *In Search Of The Real Bill Gates*. In *Time Magazine, Monday January 13, 1997.* Available online at
http://content.time.com/time/printout/0,8816,1120657,00.html, accessed May 13, 2015.

estimated $24 Billion. On his website he unashamedly advertises, "What faith is George Soros? He identifies himself as an atheist."[2] Warren Buffett is the third richest man in the world. When once receiving a letter asking what his religious beliefs were, he is reported as having simply wrote back "Agnostic".[3] Stan Lee is one of the most successful writers of all time. When asked if there was a God his answer was "I really don't know. I just don't know."[4]

All this is not to say that these men will never find God (I hope they do) but the point is that by having a life of ease they are not being pushed to seek and find God to help them through their troubles. Rather than being a blessing, these men's wealth has actually turned into a curse because it has kept them from being in the position to where they had nowhere else to turn to for help but God. The plain and simple truth is that the easier a life a person has, the less likely they are to find God.

Jesus made mention of this when He taught His disciples on being rich.

> Then Jesus said to His disciples, "Assuredly, I say to you that **it is hard for a rich man to enter the kingdom of heaven**. And again I say to you, it is easier for a camel to go through the eye of a needle than for a rich man to enter the kingdom of God." Mat 19:23-24NKJV

It's not that automatically having wealth keeps us from Heaven (as if money in and of itself was sinful) but when we have something other than God to trust in, we will often trust in it (place our faith in it as our source of sustenance and help) rather than God.

Simply put, don't be jealous of people who have an easy, perfect life because those people will never find God. Be thankful that God has taken the steps to send things into your life to prod

[2] *George Soros Faqs: The Official Resource For Information On George Soros: Religion.* Available online at http://www.georgesoros.com/faqs/entry/georgesorosviewsonreligion/, accessed May 13, 2015.

[3] *Warren Buffett*, Philosopedia entry. Available online at http://www.philosopedia.org/index.php/Warren_Buffett, accessed May 13, 2015.

[4] Stephen Thompson. *Is There A God?* October 9, 2002. Available online at http://www.avclub.com/article/is-there-a-god-1413, accessed May 13, 2015.

you into finding Him and realize that you are more fortunate than the world's wealthy elite.

Living Life With No Complaints

The Bible says that Christians are not supposed to complain (even when we are having a bad day).

Do all things without complaining and disputing... Php 2:14NKJV

...nor let us tempt Christ, as some of them also tempted, and were destroyed by serpents; nor complain, as some of them also complained, and were destroyed by the destroyer. 1Co 10:9-10NKJV

Instead, we are actually supposed to thank God for *everything* that is happening in our lives (even the bad days).

In every thing give thanks: for this is the will of God in Christ Jesus concerning you. 1Th 5:18KJV

I know what you are thinking—*Are we supposed to give thanks to God for everything that happens to us?* Flat tires? Getting fired? Marriage falling apart? Well, if we are honest, we will admit that that is what the Bible says. In the natural (i.e. non-faith) world being thankful for bad things doesn't make very much sense. But if we believe that God is in control of all of the bad things that are happening to us *and* believe that He is using them to ultimately bring about good into our lives it begins to make sense. Looking at life like this is really *the only* way that a person can stop complaining and start giving thanks for everything in their life from their heart. If we have faith it makes sense to not only stop complaining and start giving thanks but to do it with gladness in our hearts. But if we don't have faith, when we read something like this it's just not going to make sense. From a natural perspective, why would we be thankful for something bad that has happened? It doesn't make sense to do that. But once we realize that *all* of our negative circumstances were orchestrated by God and put there to ultimately bring good blessings into our lives, we won't be able to resist thanking and praising Him no matter what we are going through.

Feeling Good No
Matter Who Wins The Election

Since we are talking about complaining this is probably a good place to talk about how we should feel when our candidate of choice loses the election. After every election I dread logging into Facebook because I know that many of my Christian friends will be expressing their lack of faith over the election results. Their posts let me know that they haven't accepted that God controls everything, including election results. The Bible clearly shows that political leaders are in the places of authority that they are in because God has decided to put them there:

Let every person be subject to the governing authorities. For **there is no authority except from God, and those that exist have been instituted by God**. Therefore whoever resists the authorities resists what God has appointed, and those who resist will incur judgment. For rulers are not a terror to good conduct, but to bad. Would you have no fear of the one who is in authority? Then do what is good, and you will receive his approval, for he is God's servant for your good. But if you do wrong, be afraid, for he does not bear the sword in vain. For he is the servant of God, an avenger who carries out God's wrath on the wrongdoer. Therefore one must be in subjection, not only to avoid God's wrath but also for the sake of conscience. Rom 13:1-5ESV

Paul tells us that "there is no authority except from God, and those that exist have been instituted by God". Jesus reconfirmed this when He stood before Pilate, explaining to him that God controlled everything that happened in the world:

Therefore, when Pilate heard that saying, he was the more afraid, and went again into the Praetorium, and said to Jesus, "Where are You from?" But Jesus gave him no answer. Then Pilate said to Him, "Are You not speaking to me? Do You not know that I have power to crucify You,

36

and power to release You?" Jesus answered, **"You could have no power at all against Me unless it had been given you from above**." Jhn 19:8-11aNKJV

As Jesus stood before Pilate He had no fear of what he would do to Him but calmly told him that he would not be in a position of authority over Him unless God had placed him there. The same is true for every elected official. God decides who wins and loses every election that happens and puts the people in place (some good, some bad) that He wants there to achieve His purposes on the earth. It is unbiblical to think that God only wants righteous people to fill every office as God will sometimes put an unrighteous person in office and then use them to magnify His name:

For the Scripture says to the Pharaoh, "For this very purpose I have raised you up, that I may show My power in you, and that My name may be declared in all the earth." Rom 9:17NKJV

So there is never any reason to complain or be discouraged over the results of an election. God's purpose will stand no matter who wins or loses and, ultimately, the *only* person who gets that position is going to be the *only* person God wants to have that position. And, best of all, God will get the glory no matter who wins or loses because He is working everything together for His perfect plan. So, let's not be discouraged come the next election but no matter who wins put on Facebook that God is in control and going to use whoever won for His purposes.

Patience

The Bible says that we should be patient in our circumstances, whatever they may be.

Rest in the LORD, and wait patiently for him. Psa 37:7aKJV

We urge you, brethren, admonish the unruly, encourage the fainthearted, help the weak, **be patient with everyone**. 1Th 5:14NASB

37

What? You want me to be patient with that coworker who constantly gets on my nerves? You don't want me to express any frustration when the cashier is moving exceptionally slow and I am already behind schedule? You want me to remain calm, cool and collected, when my car won't start and I need to get to work? You want me to keep my composure when my son has just accidentally knocked over our prized China cabinet? Well, as in our last section, that is what the Bible says. God says that He wants us to be patient towards everybody in *all* circumstances. But how can we do this? The answer lies simply in having faith that *whatever* trying circumstance you find yourself in that God has not only designed it specifically for you but did so to ultimately bless you.

When we remember that our trials are designed to bring us closer to God we endure through them much more easily and successfully. If our circumstances were left up to chance or fortune it would make no sense to have patience during our trying times. But the fact that we know God is in complete control and guidance of everything that we are going through means that not only can we have patience but it is also *logical* to do so. Why lose your patience when you know that God is in control and is working the circumstance for your good? Losing your patience in that situation is what *doesn't* make sense. Accepting the message of faith enables us to become the people of patience that God desires us to be. Simply put, we will have patience once we believe that a good God is in control of our lives. Until then we will struggle with exercising patience.

Joy

Another area that having faith will impact is the area of joy.

Rejoice in the Lord always: and again I say, Rejoice. Php 4:4

Paul tells us that we are supposed to always rejoice. What? You mean I should be rejoicing when I looked away for a moment only to have my attention caught by rear-ending the car in front of me? You mean I should have joy when my grandmother died? You mean I should rejoice over being informed that I am being laid off? Again, according to the Bible, yes!

38

Joy is one area that people often confuse with happiness. Joy is an inner peace and contentment that gives us courage in the face of trials. Happiness is the feeling that occurs when something (or everything) is going exactly the way we want it to. There is a big difference between the two. The Bible never says that we are supposed to be happy all the time. It does, however, say that we should have joy at all times. And the answer for this, as stated before, is connected to the issue of having faith. If we truly believe that God is controlling all of our negative circumstances for our good, then the natural result will be to have joy within our hearts. It is impossible to be happy at all times, but one can have joy at all times by exercising faith.

Contentment

According to the Bible, God wants us to be content with just having our basic needs met:

And the soldiers likewise demanded of him, saying, And what shall we do? And he said unto them, Do violence to no man, neither accuse any falsely; and **be content with your wages**. Luk 3:14KJV

Now godliness with contentment is great gain. For we brought nothing into this world, and it is certain we can carry nothing out. And having food and clothing, with these we shall be content. 1Ti 6:6-8NKJV

When we want something but cannot get it, that is a clear sign that God does not want us to have it at the present time. Remember that He controls all things, including what you have and don't have. This means that if He wanted you to have it, you would have it and not having it means that He doesn't want you to have it at the moment. When that happens (and it happens to all of us) we should accept that the current situation is for our benefit and then start praying for what it is that we want. Sometimes God will keep something from us that He knows we want because He wants to teach us how to pray and receive things from Him in answer to our prayers. For some of us, having something withheld is a lesson in prayer. Until God answers the prayer, faith says that "This is just how God wants things for the time being."

Closely related to the issue of contentment is the issue of debt. We live in a debt filled society and Americans today probably have more debt now than at any other time in human history. All this takes place in spite of the fact that the Bible never says anything positive about debt but generally portrays it in a negative light. Debt is usually the result of not having faith and is actually often a person's way of trying to circumvent the circumstances that God has placed into their lives. To be clear, we are not talking about unexpected debt (such as an emergency hospitalization that incurs a hefty bill). Instead, we are talking about the conscious decision to borrow money to pay for something that one does not have the money on their own to pay for and that they would live without having it.

The reason that going into debt is antithetical to having faith is because the message of faith teaches us that God gives us how much money He decides we should have as He deems it necessary. If a person does not have the money for something, then that is God's way of saying that it isn't necessary for them to have it at this time. When a person goes into debt to pay for something that is not necessary for survival, they are essentially trying to circumvent (go around) God's plan for their lives. Going into debt can actually be a manifestation of a lack of faith because when one has faith, they become content with what God has given them. To put this simply, if there is no money for a new car, God wants you to keep driving the old one. If there is only enough money to rent an apartment, God does not want you to buy a house yet. And so forth and so on.

The decision to go into debt is often motivated by pride. People think "Why should I drive an old car?" "Why should I wear last year's suit to church?" "Why should I live in that neighborhood?" Faith offers the answer to all of these questions. If you don't have money to buy a new car, God wants you to keep driving the older one. If you have to borrow money to pay for a new suit for church, God wants you to keep wearing the older one. If you don't have money to move out of your current neighborhood, God wants you to stay there. The message of faith is that you are where you are because God wants you there! And if He wanted you to move from there, He would give you the means to do it!

We are who we are financially because God has decided that it would be so. God allots to us exactly how much money He wants us to have (down to the last penny). If you add up all of your assets, the exact amount you have is the exact amount that God wants you to have. So, don't try to circumvent God's plan for your life by going into debt. Accept that you are where He wants you to be (even if it means driving an older car and wearing an older suit to church) and be content with what He has given you. And in the meantime, if these are things that you want keep praying for a way to get them honestly and on your own.

One of the great mysteries of debt is that people do not realize how deceptive it is. People borrow money to buy a car or a house and then somehow feel like (and present themselves to the world as if) they owned the things they have purchased on credit. But nothing could be further from the truth. When you borrow money to buy something you don't own it. You are only pretending that you do. Even worse, people borrow money to buy things which they then use to give themselves value. "He drives a nice car!", "She lives in a nice neighborhood!" etc. The truth is, these people should be pitied more than looked up to because for all of their glitz and glamour they really have nothing to show other than weighing themselves down with useless debt and becoming examples of how people without faith burden themselves. Faith says "I will be content with what God has given me and wait for Him to give me more." The lack of faith says that "God has somehow made a mistake by not giving me the money to live in that neighborhood or drive that car. I will fix His mistake by borrowing the money to pay for what He surely wants me to have."

Avoiding Worry

Jesus said that we should never worry:

Therefore I say to you, **do not worry about your life**, what you will eat or what you will drink; nor about your body, what you will put on. Is not life more than food and the body more than clothing? Look at the birds of the air, for they neither sow nor reap nor gather into barns; yet your heavenly Father feeds them. Are you not of more value than they? Which of you by worrying can add one cubit to his stature? So why do you worry about clothing? Consider

41

the lilies of the field, how they grow: they neither toil nor spin; and yet I say to you that even Solomon in all his glory was not arrayed like one of these. Now if God so clothes the grass of the field, which today is, and tomorrow is thrown into the oven, will He not much more clothe you, O you of little faith? Therefore **do not worry**, saying, 'What shall we eat?' or 'What shall we drink?' or 'What shall we wear?' For after all these things the Gentiles seek. For your heavenly Father knows that you need all these things. But seek first the kingdom of God and His righteousness, and all these things shall be added to you. **Therefore do not worry about tomorrow, for tomorrow will worry about its own things**. Sufficient for the day is its own trouble. Mat 6:25-34NKJV

Again, we are left to say "Wow!" How can a person possibly live without worrying? The answer, as with all of our other hard verses lies in *faith*. When we see all of the events of our lives (whether they are good or bad) as carefully orchestrated and planned specifically for us by a loving Creator who is going to use them to only help us, we realize that we do not have to worry. If life is left up to chance or happenstance then it would be a little more understandable to worry (although it still wouldn't change anything). But since the Scriptures show us that there is no such a thing as chance or happenstance, it becomes easy to see why we do not have to ever worry—*God is in control and He is working everything out for our best if our hearts are set on serving Him (Rom 8:28).*

Looking at trials as bad things instead of blessings to help us leads to anxiety and worry. That is just the natural result of not having faith. And anxiety and worry can ultimately lead to psycho-anxiety problems and the decision to start taking medication for them. In reality, much of what is diagnosed as mental illness in our times is actually the result of not having faith. The sad truth is that if we do not have the faith that ALL THINGS are working for our good, then this will lead to anxiety, stress and possible mental breakdowns that will result in either hospitalization or medication or both! And no one wants that. And God doesn't want you to experience that either. That is why He gives us faith, so that we don't have to become stressed out and allow worry to hurt us.

Having faith will lead to internal peace. Contrariwise, having anxiety and worry is the evidence that we do not have faith like we should. The more faith a person has, the less anxiety they will have. Exercising faith will always lead to patience, tranquility, peace and freedom from worry.

Life can be seen like two passengers taking a ride on a train. One passenger trusts the conductor. He has the confidence in him that he will only make the right decisions for his journey to ensure that he arrives at the right destination at the right time. Even though the trip is filled with many bumps and possible delays, this passenger has a pleasant journey because he trusts in the guidance and wisdom of the conductor. Another passenger does not trust in the conductor. He views him as unwise and unskilled in driving the train and has a very unpleasant trip. Every time they hit a bump on the tracks he criticizes the conductor, accusing him of not knowing what he is doing. Every time the train slows down he gets frustrated, and even mutters that he could better drive the train than the conductor. By the time that the journey ends the second passenger is anxious, frustrated, angry and mentally wearied while the first passenger is at peace, content and able to focus on arriving at his destination.

In life we are going to be like these passengers in one way or the other depending upon the kind of faith we have. God is the conductor of our lives and He expects us to trust that He is all wise and all skilled in how to conduct us on our journey through this life. If we are like the passenger with faith, we will trust that no matter how many bumps we hit on the tracks that God knew exactly what He was doing and had our best interest at heart. But if we don't have faith, we will be like the frustrated, worried, and anxious passenger who is miserable throughout his whole journey. Even worse, if we lack faith like the miserable passenger we may even dare to verbally criticize God, exalting ourselves above Him by saying that we know better how to conduct our lives than He does. How foolish a thing to do!

Simply put, having faith leads us to freedom from worry in our lives.

Not Fighting Back With, But Forgiving Our Enemies

Jesus had some pretty unusual things to say about how we should relate to those who don't like us:

> You have heard that it was said, 'An eye for an eye and a tooth for a tooth.' But I tell you not to resist an evil person. But whoever slaps you on your right cheek, turn the other to him also. If anyone wants to sue you and take away your tunic, let him have your cloak also. And whoever compels you to go one mile, go with him two. Give to him who asks you, and from him who wants to borrow from you do not turn away. You have heard that it was said, 'You shall love your neighbor and hate your enemy.' But I say to you, love your enemies, bless those who curse you, do good to those who hate you, and pray for those who spitefully use you and persecute you... Mat 5:38-44NKJV

Jesus begins His discourse on relating to our enemies by emphasizing that the people have heard revenge was okay (an eye for an eye) but instead we should *not put up a resistance* when people are mean to us. And He gives some very detailed discussion on this topic. He says if someone tries to sue you for something, give him that and more! If you are forced to carry a Roman soldier's belongings for one mile (a practice common in Jesus' time) go two! He goes on to say that we should do good to our enemies, bless and pray for those who hurt us. But how can we do this? Faith has the answer.

When we realize that all of the people who hurt us are *only* brought into our lives by God to help fulfil His purpose in our lives, we can live in forgiveness and patience towards them without getting revenge. The message of faith compels us to look at our enemies differently than we would in the natural. In the natural, when someone tries to hurt us, our natural instincts take over and we try to hurt them back. But when we realize that God makes the day of adversity (Ecc 7:14) and sends the bad times that we experience (Isa 45:7) we realize that we have to look at our enemies in a different light. When we view life through the faith that God is controlling *everything* that is in our lives we will begin to see our enemies as agents of God, sent by Him to help mold and shape us into the people He wants us to be. This is really all that any enemy is—Simply a tool in the Hands of God to make you and

I into the person He desires us to become. Enemies are that and nothing more. To be clear, I don't think that the people who become our enemies realize that they are as such. Remember that when a person rejects God's will for their lives, they will eventually be given over to a depraved mind and can be used by God to achieve His purposes in the earth, to their own detriment. But that is really all any enemy ever is for a person—*an agent of God in their lives for good.*

I will share a story from my own life to demonstrate this. When I spent a summer in Great Britain on a missions trip the pastor that I lived with was a terribly abusive man. He had a temper and really had a bully mentality. I always felt like he didn't like me but I was kind of stuck there for nine weeks, living in his home. Prior to going on that trip I had been more of a timid kind of person. But after living with a bully for nine weeks and realizing that bullies were really more bark than bite, I developed a new boldness in life towards other people. At the time I just thought of this man as a troublemaker and thorn in my flesh. But later, I could see how God had orchestrated the whole thing and actually used this man's abusive treatment of me to make me more into the person that He wanted me to become. Just as the message of faith teaches, what seemed like a horrible situation was actually being used by God to bless me and today I am a stronger man because of it. The same can be true of your enemies too if you will respond to them in faith according to the way Christ commands us.

This, I think, is great news for all of us. No longer do we have to feel like we are at the mercy of our enemies (especially when they have some kind of authority over us such as being a bad boss, corrupt police officer or dishonest politician). You have never been at the mercy of anyone other than God Almighty who controls all of the circumstances in your life. Your enemies can do nothing to you that God does not explicitly decide that they will do to you. He puts a hedge around you and will not allow your enemies to do anything to you outside of His plan for your life. So, don't be discouraged if God has brought enemies into your life (we all will have them at some time or another). Instead just live in patience and love towards them while you continue to pray for a release from the trial, trusting that they are a part of God's perfect plan for your life until then.

Looking at our enemies through the message of faith means that we will have more peace in our lives as we will then spend less energy on arguments and disputes with people, accepting instead that the enemy is merely just an agent in God's Hands to help us. On the contrary, living with a lack of faith will lead to just the opposite—insults, holding grudges, or, worst of all, getting revenge.

Closely related to this is the issue of forgiveness. Jesus and Paul said that we must forgive *everyone* who wrongs us:

And whenever you stand praying, forgive, if you have anything against anyone, so that your Father also who is in heaven may forgive you your trespasses. Mrk 11:25ESV

Put on then, as God's chosen ones, holy and beloved, compassionate hearts, kindness, humility, meekness, and patience, bearing with one another and, if one has a complaint against another, forgiving each other; as the Lord has forgiven you, so you also must forgive. Col 3:12-13ESV

In the natural, such a declaration doesn't make any sense. Why should I forgive those who hurt me? *I have a right to hold a grudge because I wasn't doing anything and they came along and did something to me!* But when we look at those who wrong us through the eyes of faith we realize that it makes no sense to hold onto unforgiveness. For, if the person who hurt us only did so because God wanted them to in order to instill into us some kind of character trait that we were lacking, there just doesn't seem to be any reason to not forgive. Why be angry with the person when the person really was not the ultimate one behind what was happening? It doesn't make any sense. Instead we should actually feel sorry for them that their wickedness has put them into a position to where God would use them in such a way. But only those with faith can really understand this way of looking at our enemies.

Living Without Fear

According to the Bible we should not be people motivated and controlled by fear:

46

Even though I walk through the valley of the shadow of death, I will fear no evil, for you are with me; your rod and your staff, they comfort me. Psa 23:4ESV

Don't fear those who kill the body but are not able to kill the soul... Mat 10:28aHCSB

Fear is probably the greatest motivator of humanity. People will live their lives based upon the fear of what making certain decisions will lead to. *Fear of failure...Fear of rejection...Fear of what others will think.* But having faith will help to eliminate the fear in our lives. When a person has the faith that God is controlling all things for their good (meaning that all outcomes are controlled by God, not others) they will not allow fear to control them. Instead, they will courageously step out in the faith that whatever happens is what God wanted to happen. What this means is that a person with faith will not be afraid to ask out that girl on a date as the outcome is decided by God (not the girl). A person of faith will not be afraid to share Christ with their neighbor because they know that the reception they receive is in the Hands of God, not their fellow man. A person of faith will not be afraid to do the right thing because they know that God will control the results and consequences of doing the right thing. Having faith will kill the fear that plagues humanity. Fear of man does not come from God and God does not want us to be fearful people. However, a lack of faith leads to a fear of natural objects (human and otherwise) which in the end will lead to anxiety.

Closely related to this area is the concept of flattery, a sin that is so common that people don't even seem to realize that it is a sin anymore.

Everyone utters lies to his neighbor; with flattering lips and a double heart they speak. May the Lord cut off all flattering lips, the tongue that makes great boasts, those who say, "With our tongue we will prevail, our lips are with us; who is master over us?" Psa 12:2-4ESV

Flattery is when we tell people what they want to hear so that we can get some kind of desired response or action out of them, such as when an employee is always complimenting the boss, not because he thinks he is doing a good job, but because he wants a promotion. Flattery is deception. Fear sometimes leads to flattery when we tell people what we think they want to hear out of the fear of what will happen if we speak the truth. When we have faith, we realize that we do not need to flatter other people. We can be honest with them and let them know exactly how we feel about them. To be clear, we don't always need to tell everyone what we think of them but, at the same time, it is a sin for us to praise people when we feel like they don't really deserve it and a lack of faith (manifested by fear) often leads people to do this. Having faith that God is going to control how people respond to our honesty and any repercussions that come from it gives us the courage to speak honestly and forthrightly with the people that God has brought into our lives.

Avoiding Anger

Let all bitterness and wrath and anger and clamor and slander be put away from you, along with all malice. Eph 4:31NASB

It is impossible to live life without facing situations that can cause anger and becoming angry is not always a sin (remember that even Jesus got angry on at least one occasion) but having faith can keep us from getting unnecessarily angry. When we remember that everything we face (even the situations that make us angry) are sent by God to help us become the people that He wants us to be it will help to keep us cool, calm and collected, whereas those without faith will become hot and emotional.

Anger is often a sign of spiritual laziness (although most do not realize this) in which the person is not willing to rise up to the challenges that God is sending them for their own good. Rather than accepting in faith that God wants them to have to deal with the difficulty they are experiencing as part of their spiritual growth, many people instead allow anger to flow into their hearts and spill out through their words and actions. Our trials are opportunities to grow and improve but how many look upon them *only* as opportunities to get mad?

We should also remember that people who are angry can be (without realizing it) actually angry at God. This is because

48

whatever situation it is that you are angry about happening, it is God who is the ultimate cause of it and the reason that it is happening. Therefore, to be angry about something is to actually be angry at God who is the cause of all things.

Jealousy, Envy And Covetousness

Jealousy, envying and coveting are other areas where faith will cause us to overcome the world's way of doing things.

For where jealousy and selfish ambition exist, there will be disorder and every vile practice. Jam 3:16ESV

But sexual immorality and all impurity or covetousness must not even be named among you, as is proper among saints. Eph 5:3ESV

Let us not become conceited, provoking one another, envying one another. Gal 5:26ESV

Although the three terms of jealousy, envy and covetousness are often used interchangeably as if they meant the same thing, they actually have distinct meanings. Jealousy is the fear of losing something that you feel already belongs to you. Covetousness is the desire to have something which is not yours and currently belongs to someone else. Envy is the desire to have something which is not yours and the begrudging of the person who actually possesses it.

Having faith squashes jealousy, envy and covetousness because these behaviors all result from not believing that God controls all that we currently have, whether we lose it or not, and that He controls all that we are unable to have (and all for our good). Having faith leads us to recognize that we are who we are (materially, physically, mentally, etc.) because God has decided to make us that person for our good. We might not have the wealth, health or dynamic personality that we desire but faith leads us to accept who we are with joy, pray for what we don't have but desire, and wait patiently (without covetousness or envy) until God decides to give it to us. Likewise, when we have faith we will not spend our time jealously guarding all of our possessions because we will realize that sometimes God sees it as necessary to take

49

something away from us that we own, but only in order to help us become a better person.

People who allow jealousy, envy and covetousness to well up in their heart all have unhealthy preoccupations. Those who are jealous are too focused on the possessions that God has temporarily entrusted them with (for all possession are temporary as nothing can be taken with us beyond the grave) and those who are guilty of envy and covetousness are too focused on the possessions and achievements of others. Ironically, it is often the case that the people we are covetous or envious of are actually further away from God than we are and by desiring to have their lives we can become guilty of showing a willingness to exchange the closeness we may have for God for something less.

Positive Thinking

The world is filled with negative thinkers. Everything that happens, they analyze it to find the negative and then publish the negative to the rest of the world through the medium of their complaining. If one does not have the faith that God is controlling all things in their life for their good, they are going to ultimately end up in despair and negative thinking because life will never go perfectly the way that we want it to. However, looking at our trials as events to stimulate us into becoming better people will have just the opposite effect. Instead of being negative and pessimistic people we will become positive and encouraging people.

To better illustrate this we need only look at two passengers who are embarking on their first cruise. Though unrelated they both arrive just a few minutes too late and the ship has already left the dock. As they stand there on the shore they can symbolically see their expensive cruise tickets floating out into the horizon along with the boat. The first passenger does not have faith and becomes negative, bitter, and angry and begins to complain. He sees no good in the situation because he does not believe that God is controlling all things for his own good and so he goes off miserable and proceeds to make everyone else miserable by having to listen to his complaining. The other passenger, however, has faith and as he watches the ship sailing off he just accepts that God had a better plan for him and begins to pray to ask the Lord to reveal to Him what it is that He is trying to do in his life by orchestrating it so that he missed his boat. The next day the two men read in the newspaper that the *Titanic* has sunk. At this point even the man without faith acknowledges it as a good thing and gives glory to God for sparing his life. But faith calls *all events* good things *before* anything good can be seen coming from them (it doesn't take faith to call an event good *after* one has seen the good that came from it). This is an especially important thing to keep in mind as we may never see the good for many of our trials until the next life and don't want to make the mistake of calling something God has said is good as bad.

Humility

Humility is another area that people without faith sin in.

I therefore, a prisoner for the Lord, urge you to walk in a manner worthy of the calling to which you have been called, with all humility and gentleness, with patience, bearing with one another in love... Eph 4:1-2ESV

Do nothing from selfish ambition or conceit, but in humility count others more significant than yourselves. Php 2:3ESV

Humility basically means not thinking of ourselves more highly than we should and this usually manifests itself in us esteeming others over and above ourselves. The opposite of humility is arrogance, which is a feeling of superiority over (i.e. that we are better than) others. However, when we accept the message of faith that everything we have comes directly from God (not in any way from ourselves) it instills into us a deep humility because we realize that any good thing we did was actually done by God through us, not because of any strength, talent or skill that we possessed on our own. The message of faith teaches us that everything we accomplish in this life can be traced directly back to God and looking at life from that perspective will cause us to walk in humility.

Low Self-Esteem

The world is filled with people who have low self-esteem because they do not have faith. Low self-esteem manifests itself in the form of self-persecution. When a person wrongly thinks that their success and failures are their own faults they will naturally belittle themselves in their minds. They will tell themselves things like "This is all your fault!", "You are such a loser", "You are worthless", etc. But blaming oneself comes from a lack of faith in the idea that God controls all things, including whether we succeed or fail. It is true that if we don't put forth a good effort, we probably will fail and we can't blame anyone for failure in this situation but ourselves. After all, if God has given one the ability to succeed but out of their own laziness they choose not to succeed it is their fault and no one else's. But what about those times where we put forth our best effort yet still can't seem to achieve what we desire? It is those times that the message of faith comes in to encourage us because we realize and can accept that it was God who just didn't want us to succeed and it was for our own benefit. When we look at life like this we will feel better about ourselves and our esteem will grow to a healthy level.

We should never compare ourselves to others and belittle ourselves when we don't live up to their achievements. Some people are chosen by God to do "great" things while others are not. God doesn't need everyone to be a George Washington or a Thomas Edison. And, as we stated before, these men who are deemed by history as having done something "great" only did so because God decided to use them to do the things that they did in order to accomplish His will, not because of any intrinsic ability in and of themselves. Without the grace of God guiding and empowering them to do what they did, they would have done nothing and no one would remember them today. Like others, they were tools in God's Hands to bring about His plans and purposes for the world. So, it does no good (only harm) for us to look at people like this, compare ourselves to them and then belittle ourselves for not achieving what they did. It's not meant for all of us to achieve what a select few others have. Indeed most people will never achieve anything of historical "greatness" as it isn't necessary for this to happen in order for God's plan to be brought to pass and the only reason those few people from history did was because it was God's plan, not their own.

Self-persecution and comparing ourselves to others is a prime cause of sadness, depression, and hopelessness. In most people it results from a lack of faith as people blame themselves for things which they really had little or no say so over in. God is the cause of all causes and the reason behind all reasons, including our failures. In order to overcome low self-esteem one must believe that our failures and lack of achievements are from God and are exactly what He wants, that these things are for our ultimate good, and that every failure has a reason and purpose behind it. Don't waste time beating yourself up over your failures. It does little good to ask yourself "Why wasn't I more careful?", "Why did I do things that way instead of this way?" or "Why didn't I pay attention to that?" after the fact. Asking such questions generally just makes us feel worse when it is too late to do anything about the mistake or failure. Instead of belittling ourselves, we just need to have faith that God had a reason for the failure or lack of success and that it was to ultimately make us a better person.

Staying Married For Better Or Worse

One of the most ignored teachings of Jesus in our society is that of marriage being for life. Jesus has some pretty pointed things to say about marriage, things that can be so difficult to swallow that many churches will either water them down or just avoid them altogether.

So He said to them, "Whoever divorces his wife and marries another commits adultery against her. And if a woman divorces her husband and marries another, she commits adultery." Mrk 10:11-12NKJV

Whoever divorces his wife and marries another commits adultery; and whoever marries her who is divorced from her husband commits adultery. Luk 16:18NKJV

But to the married I give instructions, not I, but the Lord, that the wife should not leave her husband (but if she does leave, she must remain unmarried, or else be reconciled to her husband), and that the husband should not divorce his wife. 1Co 7:10-11NASB

A wife is bound to her husband as long as he lives. But if her husband dies, she is free to be married to whom she wishes, only in the Lord. 1Co 7:39ESV

When many people read these verses their first reaction is to doubt that they are real. Not that they disbelieve that they are in the Bible but they seem so strict, so repressive, so difficult to follow that people just refuse to believe that God would ever impose such a "harsh" rule on humanity. "*Surely*," they rationalize, "*God would not expect me to stay in an unhappy marriage.*" But, if we are honest, we have to admit that Jesus *did say that*. These verses are in the Bible where anyone can read them, yet it seems that humanity (even many in Christianity) disagree with the idea that marriage is for life so much so that they just refuse to believe it. Untold numbers of books have been written to explain away *what Jesus said* in favor of what *he must have meant*. Still, no matter how hard people try, *these verses are still in the Bible* and I have seen many instances in which people who *would not* believe them were still convicted *after* reading them.

The message of faith really explains to us why Jesus taught that marriage was for life, whether it takes a turn for the better or worse. If God controls everything (which He does), then He controlled the circumstances that led to you marrying the person that you married (i.e., He made sure that you two met, that your paths crossed, and that you found each other attractive. He closed other relationship doors yet kept this one open and even though you may have had other relationship opportunities He made this one seem the most appealing to you). If God knows all things (which He does), then He knew the kind of person you are and any personality conflicts or difficulties that would arise after the marriage yet still caused you and your spouse to meet and find each other attractive. Finally, if God controls and uses all suffering in our lives for our good (which He does), then He wanted you to experience the bad times in your marriage that you did, in order to help you become the person He wants you to become. In other words, because God is in control of all of the suffering that you are going through that means that He is in control of *any marital problems* that you might have had.

In the natural, it would make sense to divorce our spouses and try to find someone else when we have problems with them. If your spouse is mean to you and there was no benefit to putting up with that kind of behavior, it would only make sense to divorce them and look for a better one. But once we accept the message of faith, we realize how wrong it is to divorce and replace our spouses. All suffering, *even marital problems*, come as the result of God deciding that you and I needed that to become the person He wants us to be. It has been said that God uses marital suffering more than any other form of suffering to help mold and shape character and, after seeing all of the failed marriages in our nation, I can believe that this is the most common form of suffering.

Marital problems require one to exert much more faith than problems outside of the home. This is because problems at work can be somewhat forgotten about after you leave the workplace; problems with enemies can be dealt with by avoiding the enemy; even that noisy neighbor can be drowned out by turning up the stereo volume. But problems at home with a spouse seem to follow you everywhere you go, right into your own living room!

When one is having problems with a spouse the first temptation they may have is to end the marriage. The marriage is causing the problem so the obvious answer would seem to be to end the marriage. But nothing could be further from the truth and it has been proven both psychologically and experientially that instead of ending the problems, divorce just creates a whole new set of problems that will last for a lifetime. Rather than being an end to the suffering, divorce becomes the beginning to a whole new set of strifes and problems (Who is going to get custody of the children? Who is going to pay alimony/palimony? Who will get the house? What will people think of me for being divorced? and so forth and so on). Many people, expecting the divorce to solve all of their problems, have discovered that their misery and suffering continued after the divorce and will admit that it did not provide the solution that they were hoping for.

One thing that I have noticed is that people somehow feel like finding another spouse will magically solve all of their problems. Not realizing (or refusing to believe) that God controls all of our suffering they rationalize that they just made a mistake in who they married. "I just married the wrong person," they reason "And if I can find the right person I will have a marriage made in Heaven!" The reality is that when people divorce and marry a subsequent time, *statistically most of these marriages fail as well.* This is because people do not realize that God uses our spouse to mold and shape us and if He was using the first spouse to mold and shape you, He is going to use the second one (perhaps in an even stronger way because you violated His commandment to not divorce and remarry). Once people realize this, it is easy to see why we need to stay married, even if having difficulties. And, truthfully, the Bible promises that *everyone* who does get married *will have trouble!*

Yet those who marry will have physical and earthly troubles, and I would like to spare you that. 1Co 7:28bAMP

But married people will have a hard time, and I'm trying to spare you that. 1Co 7:28bCEB

It is just that those who get married will have the normal problems of married life, and I would rather spare you. 1Co 7:28bCJB

But those who marry will have a lot of trouble, and I want to protect you from that. 1Co 7:28bCEV

But those who marry will have trouble in this life, and I want you to be free from this trouble. 1Co 7:28bERV

Yet those who marry will have worldly troubles, and I would spare you that. 1Co 7:28bESV

But I would rather spare you the everyday troubles that married people will have. 1Co 7:28bGNT

The Bible clearly states that people who get married *will have problems*, so we shouldn't be surprised when what the Bible says will happen actually does. It's just a fact of life that part of God's method for drawing humanity to Him involves allowing marital problems to occur.

Many people will ask "What about a marriage made in Heaven?" Well, aside from the fact that the Bible never promises or describes any such thing we actually do have at least three examples of marriages in the Bible that were clearly ordained by God. Because God is said to have specifically put these couples together they are, without a doubt, marriages "made in Heaven". These include Adam and Eve, Isaac and Rebecca, and Hosea and

56

Gomer. Since people seem to think that when God picks your spouse it will mean a perfect marriage let's take a look at these examples of matches made in Heaven.

- Eve caused Adam to die by introducing sin into the world and enticing him to partake in it (Gen 2:18-3:24)
- Rebecca tore apart the family by helping their son deceive his father and take advantage of his brother (Gen 24:1-67, 27:1-45, 28:1-5)
- Gomer left Hosea and committed adultery as a prostitute (Hos 1:1-9, 3:1-5)

So what we see is that every time in the Bible that a marriage is "Made In Heaven" it became imperfect, hurtful and trouble-filled. *Every time!* So take heart, if you are having trouble in your marriage that does not mean that you married the wrong person. Not at all. It simply means that God is using your marriage to draw you to Him and to make you into the person that He wants you to be. Don't be discouraged but thank God and exercise the faith that He is in control and working this out for your good. Don't believe the lie that divorcing and finding another spouse will bring an end to marital problems. It just doesn't work that way.

The question is naturally asked is there never any reason for one spouse to leave the other? Common sense tells us that in some cases, it is best for a separation to occur. Years ago I met a woman who shared with me that one day her father came home with a shotgun to try and kill her and her mother. Obviously, in a case like this, the mother could not keep living with that man and Paul addresses this in the passage from 1Corinthians which we mentioned earlier:

But to the married I give instructions, not I, but the Lord, that the wife should not leave her husband (but **if she does leave, she must remain unmarried, or else be reconciled to her husband**)... 1Co 7:10-11aNASB

Although the ideal is for all married couples to stay together, Paul knew that situations like my friend's case would and did happen and that sometimes a separation was unavoidable. In a case like that he allowed a wife to put away her husband but notice that it's not a separation to go out and find a new spouse. According the Bible, a woman in a situation like that must remain single and only has the option of reconciling with her husband, not someone else:

> ...but if she does leave, she must remain unmarried, or else be reconciled to her husband... 1Co 7:11aNASB

> A married woman is not free as long as her husband lives; but if her husband dies, then she is free to be married to any man she wishes, but only if he is a Christian. 1Co 7:39GNT

> A wife is bound to her husband as long as he lives. If her husband dies, she is free to marry anyone she wishes, but only if he loves the Lord. 1Co 7:39NLT

Remaining single or reconciling are the only options that Paul gives for a situation like my friend's. Most marriages, however, that do end in divorce do not end for reasons like the situation described above. Most spouses will never experience anything close to that and really have no justification for leaving the marriage. Initiating a separation is only allowed in the *most extreme cases* and as a *last resort*. In other words, if you can safely live with your spouse, God expects you to whether things take a turn for the better or for the worst. And, after all, that is what people normally promise Him that they will do when they get married in their wedding vows.

Understanding why God created marriage can help us to better understand why He designed it to be one that is promised to have difficulties (1Co 7:28). According to the Bible, marriage was created to be a *visible symbol of a spiritual reality*. That's a very fancy expression that basically means that God creates earthly things which give us a visible picture of things that are going on in the spiritual world. Marriage is one such symbol.

> Wives, submit to your own husbands, as to the Lord. For **the husband is head of the wife, as also Christ is head of the church**; and He is the Savior of the body. Therefore, just **as the church is subject to Christ, so let the wives be to their own husbands** in everything. **Husbands, love**

your wives, just as Christ also loved the church and gave Himself for her, that He might sanctify and cleanse her with the washing of water by the word, that He might present her to Himself a glorious church, not having spot or wrinkle or any such thing, but that she should be holy and without blemish. So husbands ought to love their own wives as their own bodies; he who loves his wife loves himself. For no one ever hated his own flesh, but nourishes and cherishes it, just as the Lord does the church. For we are members of His body, of His flesh and of His bones. "For this reason a man shall leave his father and mother and be joined to his wife, and the two shall become one flesh." This is a great mystery, but I speak concerning Christ and the church. Nevertheless let each one of you in particular so love his own wife as himself, and let the wife see that she respects her husband. Eph 5:22-33NKJV

Paul briefly mentions the comparison between Christ's relationship with the Church and a husband's relationship with his wife in the passage above. If we compare the two side by side it becomes easy to see how that marriage was created to reflect Christ and the Church.

Christ's Relationship With His Church	Husband's Relationship With His Wife
The Church is the bride of Christ	The Wife is the bride of the Husband
Christ is the head of the Church	The Husband is the head of the Wife
The Church submits to Christ	Wives are to submit to their Husbands
Christ loved the Church	Husbands are to love their Wives
Christ nourishes and cherishes the Church	Husbands are to nourish and cherish their Wives
Christ became one with His Church (Jhn 17:20-21)	Husbands become one with their Wives in the sex act (Gen 2:24, 1Co 6:16-17)
Christ sought His bride (Luk	Traditionally it is the Husband

59

19:10)	who seeks and pursues a bride
Christ left His Father to seek His bride	Man leaves his father to cling to his bride (Mrk 10:6-7)
The Church is weaker than Christ	Wives are referred to as the weaker spouse (1Pe 3:7)
Christ became engaged (betrothed) to His Church (2Co 11:2)	A marriage usually begins with a Husband becoming engaged (betrothed) to his Wife
Christ's relationship with His Church produces children (disciples, Jhn 1:12-13)	A Husband's relationship with his Wife produces children
Christ's children pass from the darkness of sin into the light of holiness (Mat 4:16)	Natural born children pass from the darkness of the womb to the light of the world
Older Churches generally do not produce converts	Older women generally do not produce children
Things are simple for new converts (1Co 13:11)	Things are simple for new-born children
Christians must mature (Heb 6:1)	Children must grow up and mature
New believers may struggle with the difference between right and wrong (Heb 5:12-14)	In the beginning children do not know the difference between right and wrong (Isa 7:16)
Babes in Christ are nourished by the Church	Children are nourished by the Wife
God disciplines His children (Heb 12:6-7)	Husbands discipline their children
The Church disciplines its children (1Co 5:1-13)	Wives discipline their children

I don't think that anyone who will objectively look at the similarities between the husband and wife relationship and Christ's relationship with His church will have any trouble seeing how marriage was a symbol for that relationship. Marriage and gender were created by God in such a way that the man represents Christ and the woman stands in the image of the Church.

That being the case we can now explain particularly one reason why marital problems exist for men. Because marriage is

60

created to be a reflection of Christ's relationship with His church, in any Christian culture (such as the United States) the marriages in that culture are going to be a reflection of what is going on between Him and His bride there. Because men stand in the place of Christ they are going to be allowed to experience from their wives what Christ is experiencing from His bride in that place. In other words, the way the Church is acting towards Christ in a given society is going to be reflected in the marriages in that society. And this will be so much so that we can tell what God thinks about His Church in a place based upon how things are going in the marriages in that place. We can explain this better with some examples.

In a society…

- Where wives commonly commit adultery it is a reflection of how the Church in that culture is unfaithful to Christ
- Where wives are independent it is a sign of how the Church in that society has become independent
- Where wives will not graciously submit to their husbands, it is an indicator that the Church is not submitting to Christ in that nation
- Where women want to live with a man but are not interested in actually getting married, it is a portrayal of how the Church in that area wants a relationship with Christ but not a committed one
- Where wives commonly leave their husbands (as in the United States where most divorces are initiated by the wife) it is a reflection of how the Church in that culture is leaving Christ
- Where wives are usually given custody of the children in a divorce it is symbolic of how the Church in that culture has taken the children of Christ (the disciples it has made) and really taken them away from Christ by not faithfully teaching and holding them to everything that Jesus taught
- Where women commonly support themselves and get pregnant outside of marriage and then raise the child by themselves it is a reflection of a Church that is living totally on its own without the desire for a relationship with Christ

As we noted in earlier sections, it's not so much that the people in these situations have no free will (we are responsible for how we behave in our marriages) but God knows how to create circumstances (via the mediums of evil spirits, angels, one-sided laws, etc.) such that unsaved men and women will follow a certain course and this course will always lead the marriages in a society to be a reflection of the Church in that society.

After writing the above I fear that it will sound like I am laying all of the blame for marital problems on wives. This is not my intention. There is no shortage of men in the world who are guilty of not treating their wives right. We live in a fallen world where there are both deadbeat moms and dads, abusive husbands and wives, and self-centered spouses of both kinds. Still, the images that God created man and woman to fulfill in the marriage relationship will always serve their purposes until marriage is no more (Mat 22:30).

If you are a man and find that you are having some of the difficulties mentioned above be encouraged knowing that your situation is not out of God's control. God has a reason for choosing you to be in the situation that you find yourself. Be patient and loving towards your spouse in your times of difficulty (whether you are a husband or a wife that is being made to suffer) and realize that your spouse is not so much an enemy as they are an agent of God to help draw you closer to Him.

I will add here one more area that men suffer in particularly with the hopes of showing how that faith can help even in this area. That is the area of the frequency and fulfillment of sexual intercourse. Men often complain of being disappointed or dissatisfied with their wife's desire for intercourse. Women, on the other hand, cannot seem to understand why it is so important to their husbands. God controls even this area of marital dissatisfaction as part of His making it a visible symbol for Christ's relationship with the Church. Just as Christ desires intercourse with His Church (via prayer, praise, worship and obedience) so man has been given a great desire for intercourse with his wife. The Church, however, does not really seem to understand this and prayer, praise, worship and obedience are often neglected leaving Christ feeling unfilled, dissatisfied and disappointed with His Church. Because women reflect the Church God has created them with a lesser sex drive than men to reflect this issue between Christ and the Church. In societies where Christ is less satisfied with His Church, the men in those societies will find that they are less satisfied in their sexual relations with their wives. The disappointment that a husband feels in this kind of situation is a mirror for what Christ feels when His church is neglectful of seeking intimate time with Him and gives men an emotional connection to the heart of Christ to help them feel what He feels.

Along these lines I will add here that there are some who believe that the relationship between a husband and wife can also be used as a measuring stick of the opposite spouse's relationship with God. This is based on Genesis 2:18 where it says that God would make Eve as a helper who "corresponded with" or was "comparable to" Adam. This interpretation believes that the way our spouse treats us will be a reflection of how we are treating God (that is, that their treatment of us *corresponds with* or is *comparable to* our treatment of God). If we are unfaithful to God, He may allow our spouse to become unfaithful to us. If we are neglectful of God, He may allow our spouse to neglect us. If we wrongly blame God and accuse Him of doing things that He didn't do, our spouses may do the same to us. I would not want to say that this was the case in every marital situation but I do believe that sometimes it is the case. A wise spouse will look at the actions of their significant other and instead of getting angry with them reflect on their own attitudes and behavior towards God to see if what they are experiencing is just a reflection of their own heart and attitude towards Christ.

Lack Of Faith Is The Root Of Sin

Having looked at the relationship between faith and obeying some of the more "difficult" commandments in the Bible we realize that faith is what leads us to trust in Christ and live as He has commanded us to. When we don't have faith it leads to complaining, discontentment, jealousy, envy, covetousness, worry, fighting with our enemies, pride and divorcing our spouses to marry someone else. James reminds us that faith must produce works in order for it to be saving faith (Jam 2:14-26) and the more we trust that God really is in control of everything that is happening to us the more willing we will be to obey Him, even when it doesn't make sense to an unbelieving world. The bottom line is that having faith will lead us to live differently than those who do not have faith. It will help us to rise above the world and live on a higher level, a level which those who refuse to believe will never understand (1Co 2:14).

Chapter 7:
Why Suicide Is Not The Answer

People who go through intense suffering will sometimes make the drastic decision to end the suffering by suicide. In fact, in the United States, every 12 minutes and 48 seconds another person makes this foolish decision. When faced with suffering, suicide is never, (*I repeat, Never!*) the answer to suffering and is actually a moral wrong that results from not exercising faith. Please note that when I refer to suicide in this section I am not talking about people who, perhaps, have a genuine mental illness that plays a part in them taking their own lives. I am talking about normal people who become so despondent over their sufferings that they decide to take matters into their hands and "fix" the problem. From a natural perspective suicide would make sense in a situation where there seemed to be no hope. However, since the message of faith *offers hope for all situations*, we realize that there is never a justification for taking one's life in an attempt to escape problems. Here are some thoughts to ponder regarding suicide.

First, remember that God wants you to have the problems that you are going through as His method of molding and shaping you. Suicide, then, is a rejection of God because instead of accepting God's will for their life, the person is attempting to circumvent His will in their own strength. This, and this alone, should be enough to let people see why suicide is such a wicked choice to make. It is basically telling God to His face that you don't want Him to accomplish in your life what He is accomplishing through your sufferings.

Secondly, suicide is not going to take you away from God's ability to cause you suffering. God can, and does, cause people to suffer after death. The only difference is that suffering in this life can lead to eternal life whereas suffering after death will *never* lead to eternal life. In this sense, we see that suicide never ends the problem. It just gives the person a whole new and eternal one to deal with.

Finally, suicide is an extremely selfish act to commit. Not only is it selfish towards God by pretending that you own your life and have the right to end it when you want to but it also is selfish towards your friends and family who will be left behind to deal with the hurt that you leave them.

If you have had thoughts about suicide, rebuke these thoughts and put them out of your mind. Have faith that God is in control of your situation, is using it for your good and that you will ultimately reap spiritual blessings from it. Then focus on seeking God to find out what it is that He is trying to instill into you through the suffering. By doing this you will be taking your focus off of the suffering (which is causing you the despondency) and putting it on God (who has sent the suffering to draw you to Him).

Chapter 8:
Sharing In The Sufferings Of Christ

Since at least the 1960's there has been a theological movement in Christianity which teaches that Christians are not supposed to suffer and that if a Christian does suffer, it's because they do not have *enough* faith. Nowhere in the Bible does it offer us a promise of escape from all problems or a life of ease once we have faith. Instead, just the opposite is actually promised and I can easily demonstrate this.

Before we look at the Bible's promise that *you will suffer* I have to first give the background on why Christians will experience a special portion of suffering in this life. According to the Bible Jesus Himself experienced a lot of suffering.

From that time Jesus began to show to His disciples that He must go to Jerusalem, **and suffer many things** from the elders and chief priests and scribes, and be killed, and be raised the third day. Mat 16:21NKJV

Notice that it says Jesus not only suffered but that He suffered "many things". He did not have just a little suffering but experienced many hardships, difficulties, and hurtful experiences. This type of treatment was one of the signs that the prophets had given so that people could recognize the Messiah when He came.

Thus has God fulfilled what He foretold by the mouth of all the prophets, that His Christ (the Messiah) should undergo ill treatment *and* be afflicted *and* suffer. Act 3:18AMP

This concept that the Messiah, when He came, would suffer was so important in helping to identify Him that Paul would bring this point up when he preached.

Then Paul, as his custom was, went in to them, and for three Sabbaths reasoned with them from the Scriptures, explaining and demonstrating that the Christ **had to suffer** and rise again from the dead, and saying, "This Jesus whom I preach to you is the Christ." Act 17:2-3NKJV

Therefore, having obtained help from God, to this day I stand, witnessing both to small and great, saying no other things than those which the prophets and Moses said would come—**that the Christ would suffer**, that He would be the first to rise from the dead, and would proclaim light to the Jewish people and to the Gentiles. Act 26:22-23NKJV

When Christ came He was God in the flesh (Jhn 1:1, 14), having laid aside His divinity (Php 2:5-8) to become like you and I so that He could sympathize and relate to and with us. In every sense of the word He was fully man just like you and I (Heb 2:16-18). Therefore, just like you and I, He had to be drawn to God the same way we are—*through suffering*. This suffering was used in the human life of Christ to teach Him who God was and how to be in relationship with Him, just like it is used for you and I. In speaking of how God used suffering to draw the human Jesus unto Himself the author of Hebrews explains:

Though he was a Son, yet he learned obedience by the things which he suffered. Heb 5:8

Just like you and I have to learn obedience through suffering, so Christ was drawn towards God through the sufferings that God orchestrated and designed for His life. One lesson to be gained from this is that everyone suffers with the intent that they will be drawn to God, even the Spotless Son of God.

When Christ lived on the earth He *suffered* to the point of death (part of the same suffering common to all mankind since the sin of Adam) but unlike others He was victoriously resurrected from death to live again and to rule over the world (Mrk 16:1-7, Mat 28:18, Rev 11:15). And this was done by God as a visible sign of His promise that one day He would resurrect all of humanity for Judgment Day (Act 24:15, 1Co 15:12-22, 2Co 5:10). Those who have lived righteously will be resurrected to experience ecstasy, peace and pleasure forevermore (Rom 2:7). And not only that, but just as Christ will become Emperor of the world upon His return, so those who have followed Him will also be given the privilege of

68

reigning with Him (2Ti 2:12, Rev 1:4-6). Those who have lived wickedly will be resurrected to experience suffering, in some form, in the lake of fire (Rom 2:8-9, Rev 20:11-15).

We all want to share in the resurrection of Christ that leads to ecstasy and pleasure forevermore but the Bible declares that if we want to share in this resurrection to a new *future* life, we must share in the sufferings of Christ in this *present* life.

> The Spirit Himself bears witness with our spirit that we are children of God, and if children, then heirs—heirs of God and joint heirs with Christ, **if indeed we suffer with Him, that we may also be glorified together**. Rom 8:16-17NKJV

> This is a faithful saying: For if we died with him, we shall also live with him: **If we suffer, we shall also reign with him**: if we deny him, he also will deny us: 2Ti 2:11-12

Notice that Paul says, "**if** we suffer, we shall also reign with him". You see, if we want to share in the victorious, resurrected life of Christ, we must also share in the hurtful, disappointing life of sufferings that He experienced. This is referred to as *sharing in the sufferings of Christ*. This might be surprising for some, especially those who have become Christians and been told that their sufferings are the result of not having enough faith but the Bible clearly says that Christians should *expect* to suffer.

> I have said these things to you, that in me you may have peace. In the world you will have tribulation. But take heart; I have overcome the world. Jhn 16:33ESV

Jesus promised us that "In the world **you will** have tribulation". It's a guarantee and there is no way to get around it. Christians should not be surprised when they have troubles in the world. That's just the way it is. You are going to have trouble, no matter how much faith you have.

> Yes, and all who desire to live godly in Christ Jesus will suffer persecution. 2Ti 3:12NKJV

The Bible promises us that **all** who try to live the way Jesus taught the world to live are going to have problems as a result. It doesn't matter how much faith you have, some suffering as a result of being a Christian is just unavoidable. And the Bible clearly states that it is only through *much suffering* that we are going to enter the Kingdom of God.

And when they had preached the gospel to that city and made many disciples, they returned to Lystra, Iconium, and Antioch, strengthening the souls of the disciples, exhorting them to continue in the faith, and saying, "**We must through many tribulations enter the kingdom of God**." Act 14:21-22NKJV

No one goes to Heaven with an easy, care free life. It is only through "many tribulations" that a person is going to make it to eternal life. So, if you are experiencing a lot of problems in life as a Christian, take heart. If you are living the way that Christ said to live you are headed towards eternal life, as evidenced by your tribulations.

As much as we would like a care free, easy life the Bible says that, as Christians, we are appointed to have afflictions and sufferings:

Therefore, when we could no longer endure it, we thought it good to be left in Athens alone, and sent Timothy, our brother and minister of God, and our fellow laborer in the gospel of Christ, to establish you and encourage you concerning your faith, that no one should be shaken by these afflictions; for you yourselves know that **we are appointed to this**. For, in fact, we told you before when we were with you that **we would suffer tribulation**, just as it happened, and you know. 1Th 3:1-4NKJV

For to you it has been granted on behalf of Christ, not only to believe in Him, but also to suffer for His sake... Php 1:29NKJV

You see, God has decided that all who are going to reign victoriously with Christ must also first suffer defeat with Him in some way. That is just how it works. This is why Paul compared our Christian walk to that of sheep being led to the slaughter:

Who shall separate us from the love of Christ? Shall tribulation, or distress, or persecution, or famine, or nakedness, or peril, or sword? As it is written: "For Your sake **we are killed all day long; We are accounted as sheep for the slaughter**." Yet in all these things we are more than conquerors through Him who loved us. Rom 8:35-37NKJV

The Christian life is just not going to be easy, no matter how much faith one has. But, just as the suffering of non-Christians is designed to draw them to God, so the suffering of Christians also works for the good in their lives:

And we know that all things work together for good to those who love God, to those who are the called according to His purpose. Rom 8:28NKJV

To continue showing that it's not true that having faith means that all suffering will disappear from our lives we can look at a few more verses.

Paul commended the Thessalonians for having faith *at the same time* they were having persecutions and tribulations:

We are bound to thank God always for you, brethren, as it is fitting, because your faith grows exceedingly, and the love of every one of you all abounds toward each other, so that we ourselves boast of you among the churches of God for your patience and **faith in all your persecutions and tribulations** that you endure… 2Th 1:3-4NKJV

The Thessalonians *had faith* but it didn't stop them from having persecutions and tribulations. Rather than faith stopping all suffering, it can actually be the opposite. People can have faith but then sufferings come anyway and they then *lose* their faith:

And when they had preached the gospel to that city and made many disciples, they returned to Lystra, Iconium, and

Antioch, strengthening the souls of the disciples, **exhorting them to continue in the faith**, and saying, "We must **through many tribulations** enter the kingdom of God."
Act 14:21-22NKJV

Paul knew that having faith would not stop all suffering (that's just not Biblical) but he was concerned that people who *already* had faith would lose that pre-existing faith when times of suffering came, so he reached out to his disciples to make sure that they were ready for the promised times of suffering when they came.

Finally, the great chapter on faith found in Hebrews 11, sometimes referred to as the Hall Of Faith chapter, shows us that people with *great faith* still experienced *great suffering*.

And what shall I more say? for the time would fail me to tell of Gedeon, and of Barak, and of Samson, and of Jephthae; of David also, and Samuel, and of the prophets: Who through faith subdued kingdoms, wrought righteousness, obtained promises, stopped the mouths of lions. Quenched the violence of fire, escaped the edge of the sword, out of weakness were made strong, waxed valiant in fight, turned to flight the armies of the aliens. Women received their dead raised to life again: and others were tortured, not accepting deliverance; that they might obtain a better resurrection: And others had trial of cruel mockings and scourgings, yea, moreover of bonds and imprisonment: They were stoned, they were sawn asunder, were tempted, were slain with the sword: they wandered about in sheepskins and goatskins; being destitute, afflicted, tormented; (Of whom the world was not worthy:) they wandered in deserts, and in mountains, and in dens and caves of the earth. And **these all**, having **obtained a good report through faith**, received not the promise...
Heb 11:32-39KJV

- Tortured
- Cruelly mocked
- Scourged
- Bonds

- Imprisonment
- Stoned
- Sawn in two
- Killed with swords
- Destitute
- Afflicted
- Tormented
- Wandering about in sheepskins and goatskins
- Living in deserts, mountains, dens and caves of the earth

That doesn't sound like a care-free, easy life to me. Does it to you? I don't think so but notice what it says about these *suffering* people. It clearly says, "these all...obtained a good report through faith". All of these people not only had faith but they had *so much faith* that they obtained a "good report"—a passing score from God on their testimonies as a result of such intense trials. These were truly men and women of faith and their testimonies were so good that they were recorded in the Scriptures as examples for us to follow. Still, despite having *exemplary faith*, their lives still experienced *intense suffering*. It really could not get any plainer—no matter how much faith you or I have, we are not going to be able to escape all suffering in our lives. If you look back at the testimonies of the above people, their faith did not provide an escape from all sufferings. Instead, it was their faith in an all-powerful God who ultimately was in control of their sufferings that gave them the grace to endure under it until the end. The same is true today. Brothers and sisters your faith is not going to keep you from experiencing problems. Problems are promised. You are going to suffer, no matter how much faith you have. But be encouraged because exercising faith has the power to help you endure through your trials until they are ended.

Chapter 9:
The Dark Night Of The Soul

There is an experience that Christians sometimes go through which is referred to as a "dark night of the soul". This term has come to describe an experience in which it feels as if God has just abandoned a person, withdrawing His presence from them and leaving them all alone. Many people experience this and, at least from my own experience with it during my trials, it is extremely confusing. The only way that I can describe it is that it literally felt like God just left. I didn't feel His presence in my life; I didn't feel Him speaking to my heart; I didn't feel His comfort; I just felt alone and abandoned. For me it was scary. I had never experienced such a feeling in my entire Christian walk. It was as if God just wasn't there anymore and you were all alone.

As I went through my own dark night of the soul I discovered that even people in the Bible experienced this. In the Psalms David wrote about his own experience of feeling abandoned by God when he cried out from the bottom of his heart, "My God, my God...why are you so far from helping me, and from the words of my groaning? O my God, I cry in the day time, but you do not hear... (Psa 22:1-2)." And Job's dark night was so dark that he felt like God was hiding from him: "Why do you hide your face...? (Job 13:24)." And Jesus Himself, as He hung from the cross, cried out in agony and desperation "My God, my God, why have you forsaken me? (Mat 27:46)."

Throughout history there seem to have been men and women who experienced the feeling of God just disappearing. One article that I read said that in the seventeenth and eighteenth centuries most pious souls seem to have gone through a period like this and Martin Luther once wrote that sometimes, "for a time God seems to hide, so that He may appear to have forgotten us..."[5] Looking back on my own experience of this it seems that it lasted maybe eleven months, maybe more before I started feeling God's presence again. I share my own experience and that in the above

---

[5] Luther, Martin: Pelikan, Jaroslav Jan (Hrsg.); Oswald, Hilton C. (Hrsg.); Lehmann, Helmut T. (Hrsg.): *Luther's Works, Vol. 2: Lectures on Genesis: Chapters 6-14.* Saint Louis: Concordia Publishing House, 1999, c1960 (Luther's Works 2), S. 2:105.

Scriptures just to let people know that if you ever do feel like God has just disappeared, it is normal and it does happen to people sometimes.

My experience with a dark night of the soul seemed to teach me a few things. First, I came to the conclusion that I had often interpreted the blessings of an easy life as God speaking to me. I feel like I realized that I had often assumed that a lack of problems was the voice of God speaking to me and when many of those blessings were taken away I felt like God wasn't speaking to me anymore. It's not so much that God was really speaking to me before my dark night as it was that I *felt* His presence in the blessings He sent me. Once those blessings were taken away, I felt like God wasn't speaking anymore. But I realized that using blessings as an indicator of whether God is in your life or not can be deceptive because, as mentioned earlier, God blesses even those who are living in rebellion against Him (Mat 5:44-45). So, we need to learn not to mistake His blessings for His saying that He approves of our lives.

Secondly, I learned that even if one does not feel the presence of God speaking to and encouraging their heart that does not mean that God is not there. During my dark night of the soul God actually sent an older man who had been a pastor into my life. This man befriended me and literally saved my life by becoming a constant source of encouragement to me during this time. I would see him almost every day and we had so much in common that I know God orchestrated his life and mine so that, for one reason, he would meet me and help to carry me through this dark time of my life. Even though I did not feel God speaking to me directly, I know that He was speaking to me through this man.

The lesson to be learned here is that if you ever do feel like God has abandoned you, don't stop seeking Him. Just keep praying, reading the Bible and fasting (as able) until you feel Him again. He hasn't left you, it only feels that way and your perception of His presence will return again.

Chapter 10:
How To Seek God

I have emphasized throughout this book that suffering is God's way of drawing us to Him. The natural question to ask is, "How do we draw closer to Him in response to our sufferings?" There are five ways that we do so: prayer, reading the Bible, repentance, fasting, and baptism.

Prayer

The most natural response when one suffers is to begin praying to ask God for help with the trouble. God desires a relationship with humanity and no healthy relationship can exist without communication. Prayer is really just communicating with God. When many people think of prayer they imagine some long, drawn out, poetical speech filled with Thee's and Thou's. Others associate prayer only with requests. They view God as a Being who is only interested in hearing what we want from Him. (But how long would you want to be friends with someone who only asked you for favors? And would you really consider a person a friend if you had to always speak eloquently to them and couldn't be yourself?)

God wants you to get to know Him and you do this partly by sharing about your life with Him. He already knows all about you (your hurts and disappointments, your strengths and weaknesses). He has been watching you ever since you were born and even before that He made plans for your life. And He wants to hear what you think about those plans. If you are not happy with something God has brought into your life, He wants you to come to Him and talk to Him about it. In fact, the reason you have those things in your life that you are not happy with is because God sent them to encourage you to come and talk to Him about them.

Be anxious for nothing, but in everything by prayer and supplication, with thanksgiving, **let your requests be made known to God**... Php 4:6NKJV

Therefore humble yourselves under the mighty hand of God, that He may exalt you in due time, **casting all your care upon Him**, for He cares for you. 1Pe 5:6-7NKJV

God wants to hear everything about us. If it's important to you, it's important to God! We should never feel bad about talking to God about anything. If it's on our hearts, He wants to hear about it (even things that we normally wouldn't talk to others about). Incidentally, He already knows everything so there is no reason to feel ashamed or embarrassed to talk to Him about any topic (even thoughts you have about sex).

Prayer, like anything else, is a discipline. One must make a conscious effort to pray, setting aside time to do it like one would any other activity. I recommend that you try to pray for about an hour every day. Many people will think, "How in the world can I do that?" For them, prayer is a struggle. They start out with good intentions, but then their mind begins to wander and before they know it they are thinking about their favorite soft drink.

There is a simple solution for this. When you are praying it is normal for your mind to wander (it happens to everybody). So, when it happens just start praying about whatever pops into your head. If your favorite baseball team pops into your mind start talking about that to the Lord, telling Him what you like about them, why you are a fan and what you hope they will achieve this season. If a movie that you recently watched pops into your head start talking to the Lord about that, telling Him what it was that you did or did not like about it. The point is, God wants to hear about what is in your heart and if things are popping into your head, it's because those things are in your heart. So don't feel bad talking to the Lord about the things that are in your heart. He wants to hear about them!

Another thing to remember is that you can pray wherever you are. One does not have to be in their closet on their knees to pray. You can pray while driving to work (just don't close your eyes), momentarily while sitting at your desk, in meetings, while on walks, lying in bed at night, etc. Basically, wherever you are, you can pray and doing so will help you to draw closer to God (Neh 2:1-6).

When praying it is necessary to talk some to God about your lifestyle. A person needs to pray and ask God if He is pleased with their life (i.e. are they living the way that He wants them to). If we have a guilty conscience, we need to talk to the Lord about that. If we read in the Bible that we are not supposed to do something and realize that we have done it, we need to talk to God about that, being honest and admitting that we have done it. This is especially important because if one will not admit their sins, they will not receive forgiveness for them (1Jn 1:9).

Through prayer, mankind is promised the ability to do the impossible:

Therefore I say to you, whatever things you ask when you pray, believe that you receive them, and you will have them. Mrk 11:24NKJV

So Jesus said to them…"I say to you, if you have faith as a mustard seed, you will say to this mountain, 'Move from here to there,' and it will move; and nothing will be impossible for you." Mat 17:20NKJV

Jesus' promise that prayer can enable you to do the impossible is a promise for everyone (including you!) but this kind of prayer experience only materializes in the life of a believer who disciplines themselves to seek God with all of their life, which involves making the effort to start and maintain a consistent life of prayer.

Reading The Bible

The Scriptures are our record of how God dealt with humanity in the past. When we read them we read the accounts of men and women who experienced and found God through their circumstances. Some of these men recorded their experiences after the fact (Jhn 14:26) while some wrote down what God specifically dictated to them as He was speaking (Exd 34:27).

The things that were written were recorded for our learning so that we could be encouraged and comforted during our time on this earth:

For whatever things were written before were written for our learning, that we through the patience and comfort of the Scriptures might have hope. Rom 15:4NKJV

When we read the stories of others who have suffered, yet still persevered in their obedience and faith to God, we are encouraged to do the same.

The Scriptures also teach us about God and what He expects of us. While we learn about God by having a relationship with Him, we also learn by studying the lives of others who had a relationship with Him. And the Bible is filled with stories of men and women who knew Him.

Through the Scriptures we learn about doctrine and see ways to reprove and correct our lives as we learn about how to live righteously.

All Scripture is given by inspiration of God, and is profitable for doctrine, for reproof, for correction, for instruction in righteousness, that the man of God may be complete, thoroughly equipped for every good work. 2Ti 3:16-17NKJV

We should try to read our Bibles on a regular basis, daily if possible, and should make it a goal to read through the whole Bible several times before we leave this earth.

Repentance

The Bible refers to a concept called repentance. Repentance is a change of mind in which a person changes their way of thinking to make it align with God's way of thinking. What this means is that if God says something is a sin, a person repents by agreeing with what God says about that behavior. If God says it is wrong, a repentant person will also say it is wrong. If God says that He hates something, a repentant person will also hate it. Once a person changes their mind about sin and starts to hate it, their life will change. If they no longer agree with a particular action that God says is a sin, they will stop doing it and encourage others to stop doing it as well. This is what the Bible means when it says *repentance*.

A person must repent in order to have a relationship with God because the Bible says that God will not hear the prayers of people who are not turning from their sins.

Now we know that God does not hear sinners; but if anyone is a worshiper of God and does His will, He hears him. Jhn 9:31NKJV

If I regard iniquity in my heart, The Lord will not hear. Psa 66:18NKJV

It's not that God doesn't actually *hear* the prayers of those who are living in disobedience to Him but that He doesn't *answer* the prayers of those who are living that way. (God hears and knows everything.) The problem is that a person just simply cannot get to know God if they have unrepentant sin in their lives—if they are living contrary to how God calls them to live:

Now by this we know that we know Him, if we keep His commandments. He who says, "I know Him," and does not keep His commandments, is a liar, and the truth is not in him. 1Jn 2:3-4NKJV

We can say that we know God all day long but if we are still living contrary to the way He tells us to live, we don't know Him. And remember, that God sends suffering, and possibly will our whole lives until we get to know Him. So, it's better to *repent* when we are young and save ourselves from experiencing extra suffering.

Fasting

Fasting refers to the giving up of something (all food, certain foods, hobbies, etc.) for a particular amount of time in order to show God how important something is to you. Fasting is found all throughout the Bible (Exd 19:15, 34:28, Psa 35:11-13, 69:10, 109:24, Dan 10:3, Ezr 10:5-6, Mat 4:1-3, Luk 2:36-37, Act 14:23, 1Co 7:5) and Jesus said that after He ascended to Heaven that His friends would fast (Mat 9:14-15).

Examples of things that a person might fast for include guidance (Jdg 20:24-28), when turning to God from a sinful lifestyle (1Sa 7:2-6, Neh 9:1-5, Jnh 3:3-5), when feeling defeated (1Sa 31:8-13, 2Sa 1:1-12), for help from God in time of need (2Ch 20:1-4), and in times of distress (Est 4:1-17).

Fasting is a great way to draw closer to God and all one has to do is decide what they are going to give up. When deciding what you are going to give up remember that you don't have to start out on a long fast when you first begin fasting. In reality, for a traditional food fast one would never want to do that but would instead want to start out slow, such as fasting from breakfast but then eating lunch. This will allow the person to gradually build up their fasting strength.

Before you begin fasting consult with a physician first to assess and discuss any health risks that you might encounter because of fasting. Not everyone is physically able to fast and God understands it if you are not able to.

Baptism

Baptism, in the Bible, is an experience in which a person is submerged under water and then raised back up to reflect their decision to associate with Christ's death, burial and resurrection.

Or do you not know that as many of us as were baptized into Christ Jesus were baptized into His death? Therefore we were buried with Him through baptism into death, that just as Christ was raised from the dead by the glory of the Father, even so we also should walk in newness of life. Rom 6:3-4NKJV

Baptism reflects the culmination of one's decision to seek, find and identify with God. When a person is baptized they are making a statement that they want to devote themselves to the teachings of Jesus, follow in His footsteps on this earth and are asking for the grace to reign victoriously with Him in the next life. Baptism, then, is seen as the fullest expression of a willingness to find God and identify with Him.

A number of things happen when we are baptized. First, we experience the life changing power of Christ circumcising our hearts:

For he is not a Jew who is one outwardly, nor is circumcision that which is outward in the flesh; but he is a Jew who is one inwardly; and circumcision is that of the

81

heart, in the Spirit, not in the letter; whose praise is not from men but from God. Rom 2:28-29NKJV

In Him also you were circumcised with a circumcision not made with hands, but in a [spiritual] circumcision [performed by] Christ by stripping off the body of the flesh (the whole corrupt, carnal nature with its passions and lusts). [Thus you were circumcised when] you were buried with Him in [your] baptism, in which you were also raised with Him [to a new life] through [your] faith in the working of God [as displayed] when He raised Him up from the dead. Col 2:11-12AMP

Secondly, we receive the precious gift of God's indwelling Holy Spirit:

Then Peter said to them, "Repent, and let every one of you be baptized in the name of Jesus Christ for the remission of sins; and you shall receive the gift of the Holy Spirit. Act 2:38NKJV

Thirdly, we receive the washing away of (remission, forgiveness for) our sins:

And now why are you waiting? Arise and be baptized, and wash away your sins, calling on the name of the Lord. Act 22:16NKJV

Baptism, then, is seen as the time and place when a person fully becomes a Christian:

For as many of you as were baptized into Christ have put on Christ. Gal 3:27NKJV

Baptism is one step towards fulfilling God's plan for a person's life and is a natural step towards seeking God when we are being drawn to Him through our sufferings.

Before closing our section on baptism I want to emphasize that baptism does not have any power in and of itself (if that were the case we could just force all of our friends and enemies to be baptized). Baptism only means something because of what God did through Christ's death and resurrection and though it has no power in and of itself, God always honors it when it is sought out by a humble and sincere heart that is seeking to find Him.

Chapter 11:
Conclusion

In closing, let's summarize what we have learned. First, God is a good God who controls everything that happens in the universe, including all of your suffering. Secondly, suffering is an unavoidable consequence of living. Everybody suffers and there is no one who is immune from it. Thirdly, suffering is God's universal method for drawing us to Him as it teaches us that we need Someone greater than ourselves to make it through life. Suffering, then, is seen to be a sign that God cares about us and wants to draw us to Him. If you are suffering, be encouraged because it means that God has not given up on you. Because God controls all things and because He is a good God, every negative experience that we have is specifically designed and orchestrated by Him to make us into the people that we need to be. Because God is good, that goodness motivates Him to only send the suffering that you and I need to become the people we need to become (never any more). If we will turn to God in response to our sufferings, He will help us to grow and change into the people that He wants us to be. Finally, God promises to remove all suffering from us if we will spend our short time in this life preparing for life in the resurrection.

If you have made it this far in the book I hope that you realize by now that your sufferings were not by chance or accident—*That the very things that motivated you to read this book (indeed, even the circumstances that put this book into your hands) were all orchestrated by a loving God who only has your best interests at heart.* Your life (including your heartaches and disappointments) are not coincidences but the evidence of a God who cares so much about you that He has directed your whole life so that it will encourage you to seek Him and eternal life through His Son Jesus. Life will always have seasons of problems, hurts and sadness but through the message of faith we can gain the courage to not only face them but to proceed towards a better resurrection in which we will totally overcome them.

Now I saw a new heaven and a new earth, for the first heaven and the first earth had passed away. Also there was

84

no more sea. Then I, John, saw the holy city, New Jerusalem, coming down out of heaven from God, prepared as a bride adorned for her husband. And I heard a loud voice from heaven saying, "Behold, the tabernacle of God is with men, and He will dwell with them, and they shall be His people. God Himself will be with them and be their God. And God will wipe away every tear from their eyes; there shall be no more death, nor sorrow, nor crying. There shall be no more pain, for the former things have passed away." Rev 21:1-4NKJV

Made in the USA
Thornton, CO
03/01/23 13:06:16

47cfc031-1029-459c-b84f-264211c4de38R01